Lovely

NICE GIFTS TO GIVE

APPLIQUÉD PILLOWS

Directions on page 49.

1

COSMETIC CASES, PEN CASE, GLASSES CASE AND SACHETS

Directions for 4 on page 51, for 5 on page 52, for 6 and 7 on page 54, for 8 and 9 on page 56.

8

9

7

POCHETTES AND TOTE BAGS

Directions for 10 on page 58, for 11 on page 59, for 12 on page 60, for 13 and 14 on page 62, for 15 on page 64, for 16 on page 65.

4

14

15

16

lovely

17

18

19

20

6

TRAY MAT, POTHOLDERS, TEA COZY, PLACEMAT AND NAPKIN

Directions for 17 on page 65, for 18 on page 66, for 19 on page 68,
for 20 and 21 on page 69, for 22 and 23 on page 70.

Let's make it

ENJOY MAKING IT

LOG CABIN BED SPREAD

Directions on page 10.

24

24 Log Cabin Bed Spread shown on pages 8 and 9

MATERIALS: Cotton fabrics: charcoal gray, 90 cm by 670cm; dark pink with wine floral design, 90cm by 190cm; pink with white floral design, 90cm by 125cm; black with white floral design, 90cm by 105cm; light pink, 90cm by 85cm; navy with gray floral design, 90cm by 65cm; fabric for interlining, 68cm by 615cm. White silk sewing thread.
FINISHED SIZE: 170cm by 234cm

DIRECTIONS: 1. Cut patch pieces adding 0.7 cm seam allowance. Sew each piece to interlining in numerical order from 1 through 12. Top-stitch by hand as shown in the illustration. 2. Following the illustration, assemble blocks together by machine taking care of placement of each block. 3. Sew pieces for lining together to make 182cm by 226cm. With right sides of pieced top and lining together and edges even, stitch along edges of each side. Turn to right side. Sew strips to top and bottom for binding.

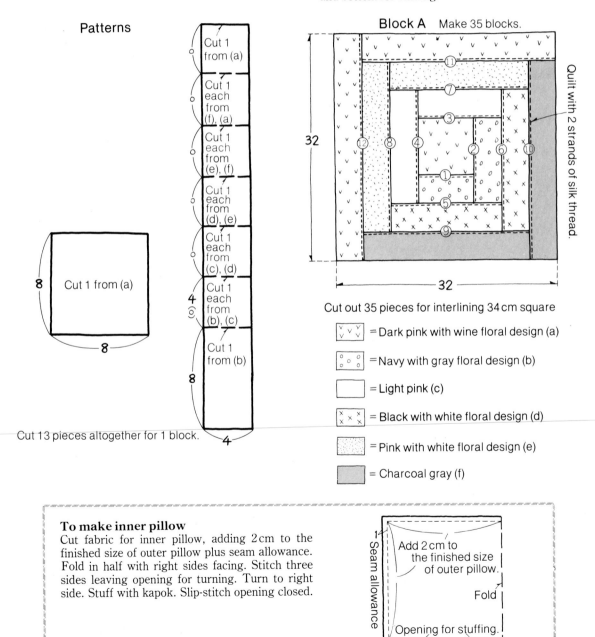

Patterns

Cut 1 from (a)

Cut 1 each from (f), (a)

Cut 1 each from (e), (f)

Cut 1 each from (d), (e)

Cut 1 each from (c), (d)

Cut 1 each from (b), (c)

Cut 1 from (b)

Cut 1 from (a)
8
8

Cut 13 pieces altogether for 1 block.

Block A   Make 35 blocks.

32

32

Quilt with 2 strands of silk thread.

Cut out 35 pieces for interlining 34 cm square

= Dark pink with wine floral design (a)

= Navy with gray floral design (b)

= Light pink (c)

= Black with white floral design (d)

= Pink with white floral design (e)

= Charcoal gray (f)

To make inner pillow
Cut fabric for inner pillow, adding 2cm to the finished size of outer pillow plus seam allowance. Fold in half with right sides facing. Stitch three sides leaving opening for turning. Turn to right side. Stuff with kapok. Slip-stitch opening closed.

Add 2cm to the finished size of outer pillow.

1 cm Seam allowance

Fold

Opening for stuffing.

To make Log Cabin block

Sew patch pieces to interlining in numerical order from 1 through 12.

①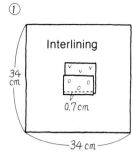

Interlining

34 cm

0.7 cm

34 cm

②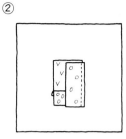

③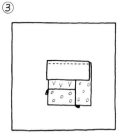

Center piece (a) on interlining.
Place piece (b) on piece (a) with
right sides together and stitch
with 0.7 cm seams.

④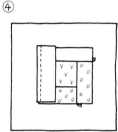

⑤

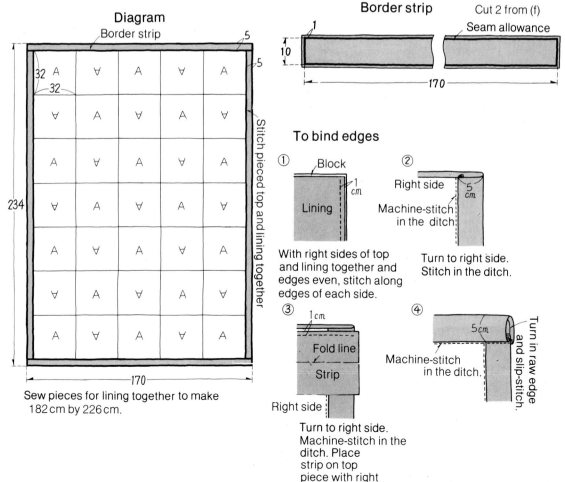

Diagram

Border strip

5

32 A   ∀   A   ∀   A

32

∀   A   ∀   A   ∀

A   ∀   A   ∀   A

234

∀   A   ∀   A   ∀

A   ∀   A   ∀   A

∀   A   ∀   A   ∀

A   ∀   A   ∀   A

5

Stitch pieced top and lining together

170

Sew pieces for lining together to make
182 cm by 226 cm.

Border strip

Cut 2 from (f)

1

10

Seam allowance

170

To bind edges

① Block

1 cm

Lining

With right sides of top
and lining together and
edges even, stitch along
edges of each side.

② Right side

5 cm

Machine-stitch
in the ditch.

Turn to right side.
Stitch in the ditch.

③ 1 cm

Fold line

Strip

Right side

Turn to right side.
Machine-stitch in the
ditch. Place
strip on top
piece with right
sides together. Stitch.

④ 5 cm

Machine-stitch
in the ditch.

Turn in raw edge
and slip-stitch.

11

MOSAIC SMALL COVERLET

Directions on page 14.

25

25 Mosaic Small Coverlet shown on pages 12 and 13

MATERIALS; Cotton fabrics: (see next page for colors and amounts for top) white with blue floral design for lining, 80 cm by 110 cm. #25 six-strand embroidery floss in cobalt blue, dark pink, white, yellow, purple and orange. Quilt batting, 78 cm by 216 cm. White cotton lace edging, 6 cm by 6 m.

FINISHED SIZE; 89.5 cm by 119.5 cm

DIRECTIONS; 1. Cut out patch pieces adding 0.7 cm seam allowance. Overcast patch pieces together, placing cardboard shape on wrong side of each piece. 2. To make ruffle, run a gathering stitch along raw edge of lace. Stitch short ends together to make a circle. Sew ruffle to pieced top. 3. Place two pieces of batting and lining on wrong side of pieced top. Turn in 1 cm seam allowance of lining and top-stitch along folded edge.

Patterns (Actual size)

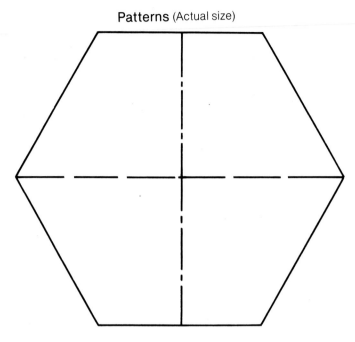

Continued from page 27.

32

Patterns (Actual size)

Diagram

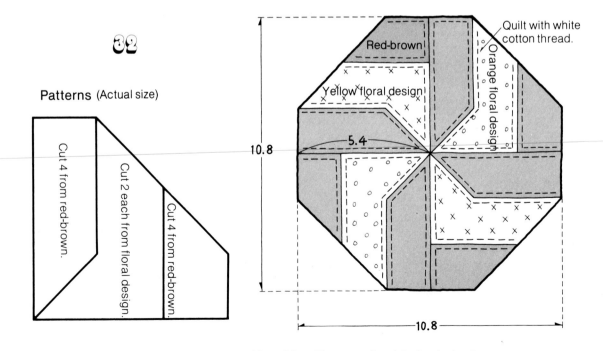

Cut 4 from red-brown.

Cut 2 each from floral design.

Cut 4 from red-brown.

Red-brown

Yellow floral design

Orange floral design

Quilt with white cotton thread.

10.8

5.4

10.8

Use white with orange floral design for back.
Cut one piece for back the size of front plus 0.7 cm seam allowance.

Diagram

Quilt on each hexagon with three strands of embroidery floss in cobalt blue.

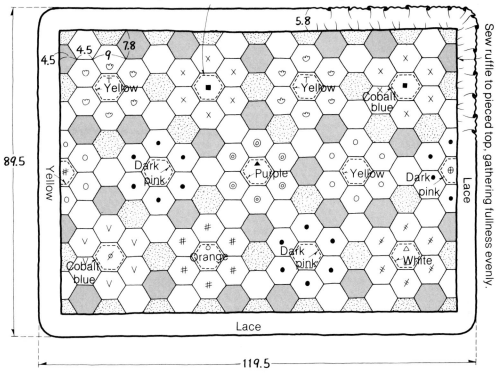

Cut two pieces 78 cm by 108 cm each from batting.

Color Key and Required Amounts of Fabrics

	Color key	⬡	⬢	◇	◇◇	Required amounts
☐	light olive green with white floral design	24	4			81cm × 40cm
▨	cream with floral design	23	4			
⠿	light gray-green print	15	14	4	Cut 2 each	82cm × 42cm
•	pink with white dots	14		2		69cm × 30cm
X	blue with white floral design	12				69cm × 20cm
♡	ivory with red floral design					
o	orange with white dots	9		2		
◎	navy with purple floral design	6				69cm × 10cm
⚡	white with red floral design					
V	white with cobalt blue floral design					
#	yellow with white dots	7		1		46cm × 20cm
⊕	dark pink	2		1		35cm × 10cm
T	red with floral design	2				23cm × 10cm
■	blue					
▲	purple					
△	red with white floral design	1				12cm × 10cm
⊘	cobalt blue with white dots					

To finish Coverlet

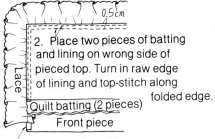

2. Place two pieces of batting and lining on wrong side of pieced top. Turn in raw edge of lining and top-stitch along folded edge.

1. Sew ruffle to pieced top.

26
Puffed Patchwork Crib Quilt shown on pages 16 and 17

MATERIALS: Cotton fabrics: (see next page for colors and amounts for top) rosepink for lining 74 cm by 1 m; back pieces for puff, 90 cm by 145 cm. Polyester fiberfill.

FINISHED SIZE: 83.5 cm by 109.5 cm

DIRECTIONS: 1. Cut out required number of pieces for puff from top and back fabrics. With wrong sides of top and back pieces together, fold extra fabric for top into a pleat and stitch all around. Following Piecing Diagram, assemble puffs by hand. Make a slash on back of each puff. Insert polyester fiberfill through slash. Overcast opening closed. 2. Stitch short ends of strips to make a circle. Fold in half lengthwise. Sew ruffle to pieced top. 3. Turn in 1 cm seam allowance of lining. Slip-stitch folded edge to ruffle.

Diagram

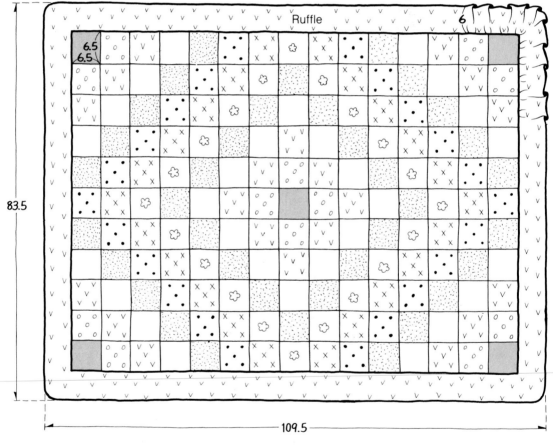

Ruffle

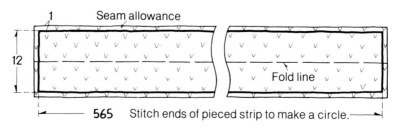

Size of puff

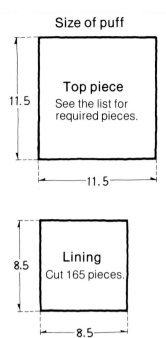

Top piece
See the list for
required pieces.

11.5

11.5

Lining
Cut 165 pieces.

8.5

8.5

Color Key and Required Amounts of Fabrics

	Color key	Required pieces	Required amounts
	pink with rosepink floral design	20 pieces for top / Ruffle	90 cm × 135 cm
	lavender	36 pieces for top	81 cm × 69 cm
	pink	28 pieces	81 cm × 46 cm
	pistachio green	22 pieces	
	gray with floral design	22 pieces	
	green with floral design (a)	20 pieces	90 cm × 80 cm
	rosepink with pink floral design	12 pieces	81 cm × 23 cm
	rosepink with floral design (b)	5 pieces	90 cm × 20 cm

Cut out pieces from (a) and (b), showing flower in the center of fabric.

To make Puff

①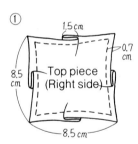

1.5 cm

0.7 cm

8.5 cm

Top piece
(Right side)

8.5 cm

Make a pleat at center
of each side. Baste.

②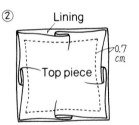

Lining

0.7 cm

Top piece

With wrong sides of top
and back together, stitch
all around. Remove basting
stitches.

③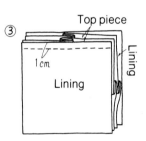

Top piece

Lining

1 cm

Lining

With right sides of two puffs
together, stitch by hand
with 1 cm seams.

④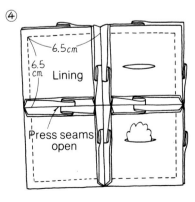

6.5 cm

6.5 cm

Lining

Press seams
open

Make a slash on back of each puff
with scissors. Insert polyester
fiberfill through the slash.

⑤

Overcast the slash closed.

⑥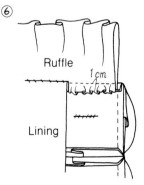

Ruffle

1 cm

Lining

Fold strip for ruffle in half. Run a gathering
stitch along raw edges. Sew gathered ruffle
to pieced top. Press seams to one side.
Slip-stitch lining to ruffle.

GIRL PILLOW AND BIRD PILLOW

Directions for 27 on page 22, for 28 on page 72.

27

27 Girl Pillow shown on page 20

MATERIALS: Cotton fabrics: white with pink floral design, 90 cm by 36 cm; pink with rosepink floral design, 90 cm by 30 cm; pink and mustard, 63 cm by 7 cm each; pale grayish wine red, 45 cm by 7 cm; pistachio green, 42 cm by 7 cm; grayish wine red, 41 cm by 37 cm; rosepink with pink floral design, and rosepink with floral design, 30 cm by 10 cm each; lavender, 18 cm by 11 cm; gray, 12 cm by 7 cm; mauve, 10 cm square; beige, 8 cm square. #25 six-strand embroidery floss in lavender, navy, black and matching colors with appliqué pieces. 30 cm long zipper. Cotton fabric for inner pillow, 76 cm by 39 cm. Kapok, 350 g.
FINISHED SIZE: 35 cm square (except ruffle)

DIRECTIONS: 1. Cut out squares adding seam allowance. Overcast squares together by hand, placing cardboard shape on wrong side of each square. 2. Enlarge appliqué patterns. Cut out appliqué pieces adding 0.7 cm seam allowance. Overcast strips for dress together, placing cardboard pattern on wrong side of each strip. 3. Turn in seam allowance of appliqués and slip-stitch to pieced front with matching embroidery floss. 4. Embroider as indicated. Cut pieces for back. Sew zipper to back. Stitch short ends of strips together to make a circle. Make two circles. Sew ruffle to front. Make up for pillow and insert inner pillow stuffed with kapok.

Pattern

Diagram
Add 1 cm seam allowance unless otherwise indicated.

Front

Back

Grayish wine-red

Zipper

Add 2 cm seam allowance

Grayish wine-red

35

35

12

23

☐ =White with pink floral design (10 pieces)

▨ =Pink with rosepink floral design (10 pieces)

▨ = Pink (9 pieces)

▨ =Pale grayish wine-red (5 pieces)

▨ =Pistachio green (6 pieces)

▨ = Mustard (9 pieces)

Ruffle
Sew strips together.

5.5

215

7.5

Bow
Cut out 1 piece adding 0.5 cm seam allowance.

Cut 2 pieces.

2

6

3

1

Opening for turning

Turn to right side   Slip-stitch at back side

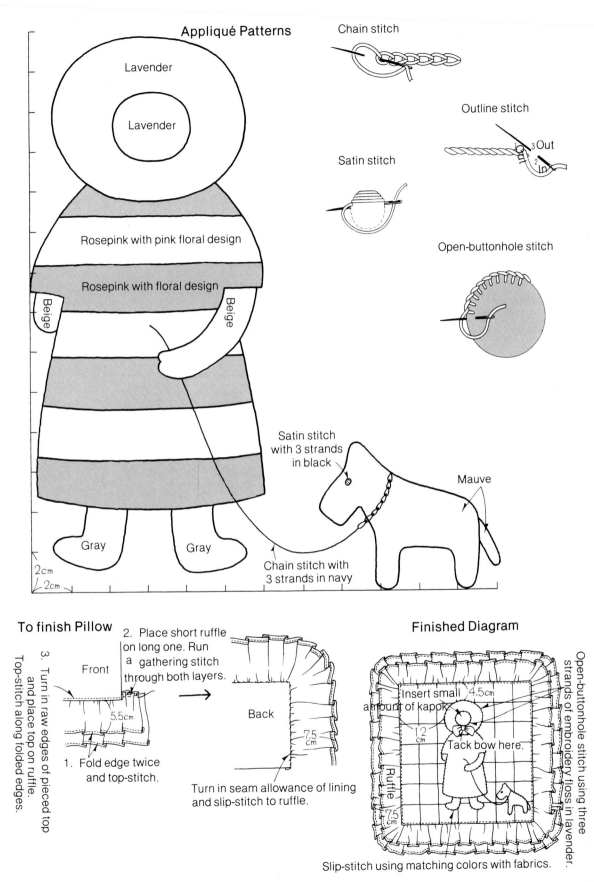

Appliqué Patterns

Lavender

Lavender

Rosepink with pink floral design

Rosepink with floral design

Beige

Beige

Gray

Gray

Chain stitch

Satin stitch

Outline stitch

3 Out
In

Open-buttonhole stitch

Satin stitch
with 3 strands
in black

Mauve

Chain stitch with
3 strands in navy

2cm
2cm

To finish Pillow

2. Place short ruffle
on long one. Run
a gathering stitch
through both layers.

Front

5.5cm

3. Turn in raw edges of pieced top
and place top on ruffle.
Top-stitch along folded edges.

1. Fold edge twice
and top-stitch.

Back

7.5 cm

Turn in seam allowance of lining
and slip-stitch to ruffle.

Finished Diagram

Insert small
amount of kapok

4.5cm

12 cm

Tack bow here.

Ruffle

7.5 cm

Open-buttonhole stitch using three
strands of embroidery floss in lavender.

Slip-stitch using matching colors with fabrics.

PIN CUSHIONS, SEWING BOX, SCISSORS AND SEWING CASE

Directions for 29 on page 26, for 30 and 31 on page 27, for 32 on page 14, for 33 on page 76, for 34 and 35 on page 74.

29

31

30

32

34

24

33

35

Let's make

29—32 Pin Cushions shown on page 24

MATERIALS: Cotton fabrics: for 29: golden brown, light blue, white with floral design and navy with floral design, 11 cm square each; navy with white floral design, 12 cm by 6 cm; fabric for lining, 12 cm square: for 30: yellow with white floral design, 21 cm by 12 cm; white with green leaf design, 16 cm by 10 cm; green with white floral design, 14 cm by 7 cm; brown with floral design, 5 cm square; fabric for lining, 11.5 cm square: for 31: brown with floral design, 14 cm by 12 cm; red-brown, 18 cm by 5 cm; white with light brown floral design, 15 cm by 7 cm; gray-green, 14 cm square; light yellow-green with leaf design, 8 cm square; scrap of yellow-green; fabric for lining, 14 cm by 12 cm: for 32: white with orange floral design, 22 cm by 13 cm; red-brown, 16 cm square; white with yellow floral design, 9 cm by 11 cm; fabric for lining, 12.5 cm square. #30 cotton sewing thread: white; navy for 29; brown for 30. Quilt batting: 12 cm square for 29; 11.5 cm square for 30; 14 cm by 12 cm for 31; 12.5 cm square for 32. Cotton for stuffing.

FINISHED SIZE: see diagrams.

DIRECTIONS: 1. Add 0.7 cm seam allowance to each piece. Sew pieces together by hand. 2. Place pieced top on batting and lining. Quilt as indicated. 3. With right sides of front and back together, stitch all around leaving opening for turning. Turn to right side. Stuff with cotton and slip-stitch opening closed. For 29, make back as for front. Cross-stitch at center using navy thread and tighten thread.

Patterns (Actual size)

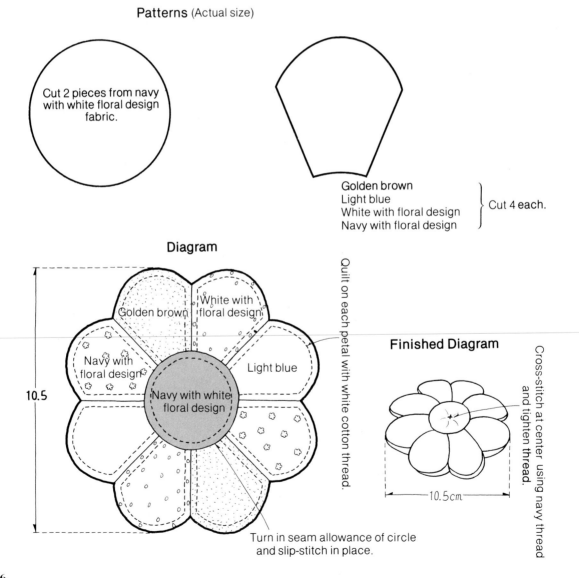

Cut 2 pieces from navy with white floral design fabric.

Golden brown
Light blue
White with floral design
Navy with floral design
} Cut 4 each.

Diagram

Golden brown

White with floral design

Navy with floral design

Light blue

Navy with white floral design

10.5

Quilt on each petal with white cotton thread.

Turn in seam allowance of circle and slip-stitch in place.

Finished Diagram

10.5 cm

Cross-stitch at center using navy thread and tighten thread.

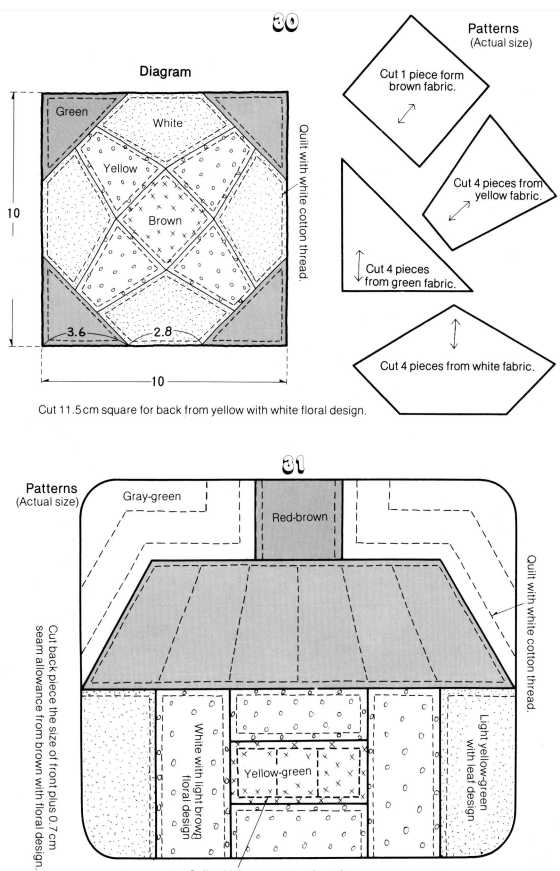

30

Diagram

Green

White

Yellow

Brown

10

10

3.6

2.8

Quilt with white cotton thread.

Patterns
(Actual size)

Cut 1 piece form brown fabric.

Cut 4 pieces from yellow fabric.

Cut 4 pieces from green fabric.

Cut 4 pieces from white fabric.

Cut 11.5 cm square for back from yellow with white floral design.

31

Patterns
(Actual size)

Gray-green

Red-brown

Quilt with white cotton thread.

Cut back piece the size of front plus 0.7 cm seam allowance from brown with floral design.

White with light brown floral design

Yellow-green

Light yellow-green with leaf design

Quilt with brown cotton thread.

See page 14 for 32. 27

QUINT
AND TWINS

Directions for 36 through 40 on pages 30 and 31,
for 41 and 42 on page 78.

36—40 Quint shown on page 28

MATERIALS: Cotton fabrics: beige for each doll, 12 cm square each: for 36: purple with white dots, 20 cm by 6 cm, pink with white dots, 14 cm by 6 cm; pink, 13 cm by 5 cm: for 37: navy with floral design, 13 cm by 7 cm; blue, 10 cm square; dark blue with floral design, 8 cm square: for 38: olive green with floral design, 13 cm by 7 cm; green, 10 cm square; white with floral design, 8 cm square: for 39: mustard with floral design and wine with floral design,• 16 cm by 8 cm each; yellow, 13 cm by 5 cm: for 40: white with floral design and red with floral design, 18 cm by 8 cm each; white, 13 cm by 5 cm. 3-ply yarn: pink for 36; blue for 37; powder green for 38; bright yellow for 39; dark pink for 40. #25 six-strand embroidery floss: blue for 37; green for 38. Black beads (medium), 2 for each doll. Kapok. Glue. Rouge.

FINISHED SIZE: Girls of 36, 39 and 40, 9 cm tall. Boys of 37 and 38, 9.5 cm tall.

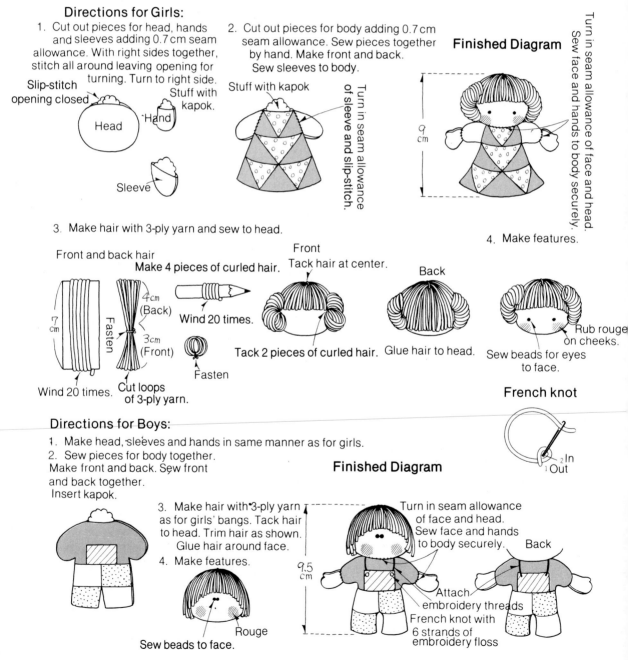

Directions for Girls:

1. Cut out pieces for head, hands and sleeves adding 0.7 cm seam allowance. With right sides together, stitch all around leaving opening for turning. Turn to right side. Slip-stitch opening closed. Stuff with kapok.

Head, Hand, Sleeve

2. Cut out pieces for body adding 0.7 cm seam allowance. Sew pieces together by hand. Make front and back. Sew sleeves to body. Stuff with kapok. Turn in seam allowance of sleeve and slip-stitch.

Finished Diagram

9 cm

Turn in seam allowance of face and head. Sew face and hands to body securely.

4. Make features.

3. Make hair with 3-ply yarn and sew to head.

Front and back hair. Make 4 pieces of curled hair.

7 cm — Wind 20 times. Fasten

4 cm (Back), 3 cm (Front). Wind 20 times. Fasten. Cut loops of 3-ply yarn.

Front. Tack hair at center. Back

Tack 2 pieces of curled hair. Glue hair to head.

Rub rouge on cheeks. Sew beads for eyes to face.

French knot

In, Out

Directions for Boys:

1. Make head, sleeves and hands in same manner as for girls.
2. Sew pieces for body together. Make front and back. Sew front and back together. Insert kapok.

3. Make hair with 3-ply yarn as for girls' bangs. Tack hair to head. Trim hair as shown. Glue hair around face.
4. Make features.

Sew beads to face. Rouge.

Finished Diagram

9.5 cm

Turn in seam allowance of face and head. Sew face and hands to body securely. Back

Attach embroidery threads. French knot with 6 strands of embroidery floss.

Patterns (Actual size)

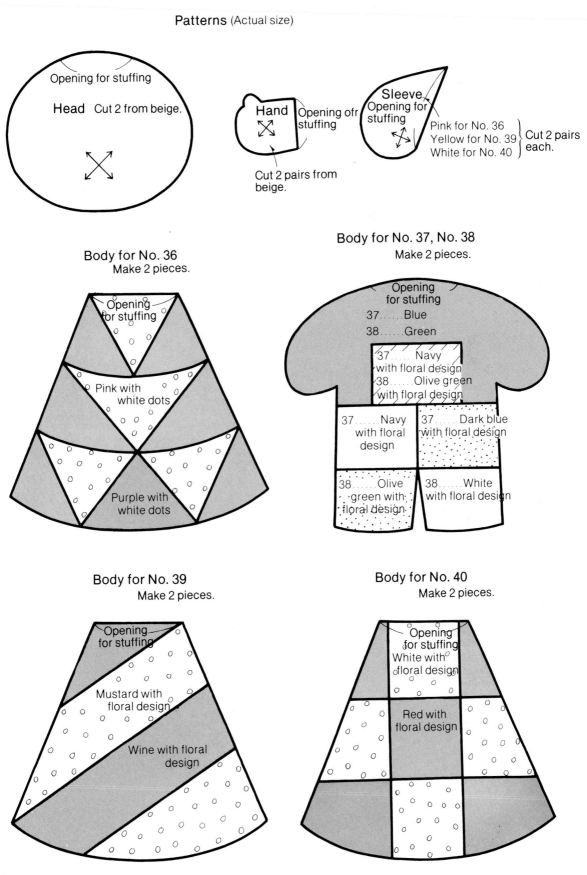

Head Cut 2 from beige.

Opening for stuffing

Hand Opening ofr stuffing

Cut 2 pairs from beige.

Sleeve Opening for stuffing

Pink for No. 36
Yellow for No. 39
White for No. 40 } Cut 2 pairs each.

Body for No. 36
Make 2 pieces.

Opening for stuffing

Pink with white dots

Purple with white dots

Body for No. 37, No. 38
Make 2 pieces.

Opening for stuffing
37......Blue
38......Green

37......Navy with floral design
38......Olive green with floral design

37......Navy with floral design

37......Dark blue with floral design

38......Olive green with floral design

38......White with floral design

Body for No. 39
Make 2 pieces.

Opening for stuffing

Mustard with floral design

Wine with floral design

Body for No. 40
Make 2 pieces.

Opening for stuffing
White with floral design

Red with floral design

CHRISTMAS TREE ORNAMENTS AND WREATH

Directions for 43 and 44 on page 34, for 45 and 46 on page 35,
for 47 on page 82, for 48 on page 83.

43 and 44   Christmas Stockings shown on page 32

MATERIALS: Cotton fabrics: for 43: green, 70 cm by 16 cm; small amount each of six different prints in red shades and green shades (see photo): for 44: green, 55 cm by 16 cm; red with white stripes, 14 cm square. Quilt batting for one stocking, 28 cm by 16 cm. Polyester fiberfill.
FINISHED SIZE: See diagram.

DIRECTIONS: 1. Cut out pieces adding 0.7 cm seam allowance. Place batting on lining. Place two patch pieces on batting and machine-stitch through all thicknesses. Place third piece on second and machine-stitch in same manner. Continue in this way until all pieces are joined. 2. Bind top edges of front piece with bias-cut strip. Make a binding for back piece, too. 3. With right sides of two pieces together, and loop for hanging in between, stitch along raw edges. Clip into curved seams. Turn to right side. Stuff with polyester fiberfill.

Patterns (Actual size)

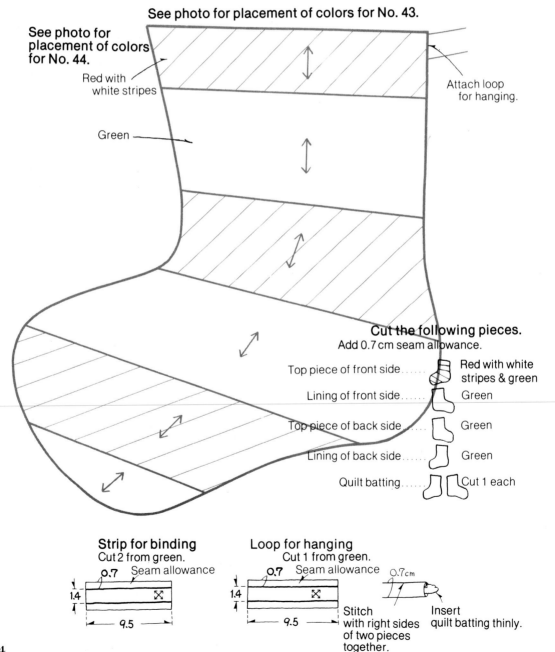

See photo for placement of colors for No. 43.

See photo for placement of colors for No. 44.

Red with white stripes

Green

Attach loop for hanging.

Cut the following pieces.
Add 0.7 cm seam allowance.

Top piece of front side...... Red with white stripes & green

Lining of front side...... Green

Top piece of back side...... Green

Lining of back side...... Green

Quilt batting...... Cut 1 each

Strip for binding
Cut 2 from green.
0.7 Seam allowance
1.4
9.5

Loop for hanging
Cut 1 from green.
0.7 Seam allowance
1.4
9.5
Stitch with right sides of two pieces together.

0.7 cm
Insert quilt batting thinly.

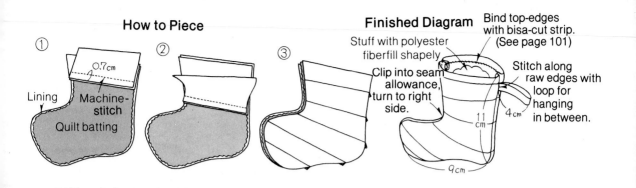

How to Piece

① Lining Machine-stitch 0.7cm Quilt batting

②

③

Finished Diagram

Stuff with polyester fiberfill shapely

Bind top-edges with bisa-cut strip. (See page 101)

Clip into seam allowance, turn to right side.

Stitch along raw edges with loop for hanging in between.

11 cm 4 cm

9 cm

45 Star shown on page 32

MATERIALS: Cotton fabrics: yellow-green with white dots, 15 cm square; small amount each of five different prints in red shades and green shades (see photo). Polyester fiberfill.

FINISHED SIZE: See diagram.

DIRECTIONS: 1. Cut out pieces adding 0.7 cm seam allowance. Sew pieces together by hand. 2. With right sides of front and back together, stitch all around leaving opening for turning. Clip into seams at corners. Turn to right side. Stuff with polyester fiberfill. Slip-stitch opening closed. Attach thread loop for hanging.

Pattern (Actual size)

Cut 5 pieces from five different prints.

Diagram

Attach thread loop for hanging.

4.5

4.5

13

Clip into seam allowance of wrong side, and turn to right side.

Cut one piece for back the size of front plus seam allowance from dotted yellow-green fabric.

46 Cane shown on page 32

MATERIALS: Red and white striped cotton fabric, 25 cm by 18 cm. Green ribbon, 1.2 cm by 35 cm. Polyester fiberfill.

FINISHED SIZE: See diagram.

DIRECTIONS: 1. Cut out two pieces adding 0.7 cm seam allowance, reversing pattern for the second piece. 2. With right sides together, stitch all around leaving opening for turning. Clip into curved seams. Turn to right side. Slip-stitch opening closed. Tie ribbon to bow. Attach thread loop for hanging.

Pattern (Actual size)

Cut 1 piece.

Cut 1 piece symmetrically.

Finished Diagram

Attach thread loop for hanging.

Tie ribbon to bow.

16.5 cm

Clip into seam allowance, and turn to right side.

CATHEDRAL WINDOW WALL HANGING

Directions on page 83.

CATHEDRAL WINDOW COVERLET

Directions on page 38.

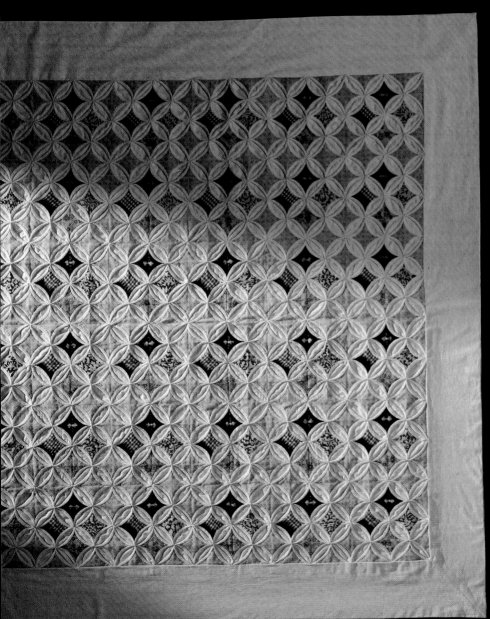

50
Cathedral Window Coverlet shown on pages 36 and 37

MATERIALS: Unbleached sheeting, 84 cm by 17 cm. Cotton fabrics: gray with design, 36 cm by 3 m; navy with design, brown with white and black checks, light plum print with maple pattern, beige with garnet red design, 36 cm by 66 cm each.
FINISHED SIZE: 134 cm by 224 cm
DIRECTIONS: 1. Cut out pieces for window patches, base and border as indicated. 2. Fold fabric for base as shown in the illustration, tacking each corner to center securely. Sew four folded pieces together to make one block. Place four window patches in different colors in place. Slip-stitch in place. Make 66 blocks. 3. Join blocks into 6 strips of 11 blocks each, overcasting edges together as shown in the illustration. Add window patches to cover all diamonds and half-diamonds with gray fabric with design. Slip-stitch in place. 4. Fold one-third of strip for border lengthwise. Refold the strip and bind raw edges of pieced top. Slip-stitch folded edges to top and base.

Cut the following pieces.
For Base

Cut out 264 pieces from sheeting.

Window Patches

Cut out 298 pieces from gray with design fabric.

Navy with design
Checks
Print with maple pattern
Beige with garnet red design
} Cut 66 pieces each.

Strip for border
Sheeting
42 cm by 137 cm for side
42 cm by 227 cm for top or bottom
} Cut 2 pieces each.

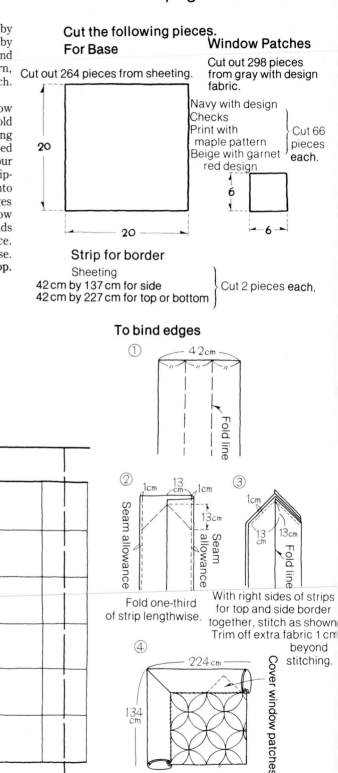

To bind edges

① 42 cm — Fold line

② Seam allowance — 1 cm — 13 cm — 1 cm — 13 cm — Seam allowance
Fold one-third of strip lengthwise.

③ 1 cm — 13 cm — 13 cm — Fold line
With right sides of strips for top and side border together, stitch as shown. Trim off extra fabric 1 cm beyond stitching.

④ 224 cm — 134 cm — Cover window patches.
Turn in seam allowance of strip. Bind raw edges of pieced top. Slip-stitch.

Diagram

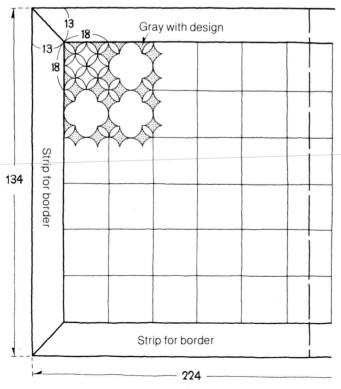

Gray with design

Strip for border

Strip for border

134

224

To make Cathedral Window

①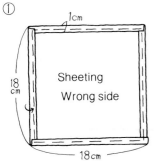

Turn over seam allowance to wrong side and baste.

1cm

18 cm

Sheeting
Wrong side

18cm

②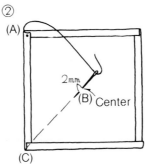

Bring the needle from corner (A) to center (B) and take a stitch toward corner (C).

(A)

2mm

(B) Center

(C)

③

Take a stitch at corner (C). Repeat in this way for remaining corners.

(D)
2mm

(C) 2mm   (E)

④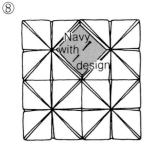

Tack corners together to center, then bring the needle out through wrong side.

(H)

⑤

Turn piece over. Refold corners so they meet at center, tacking corners together in same manner.

Right side

⑥

9 cm

9 cm

⑦

With right sides of folded pieces together, overcast along one edge.

⑧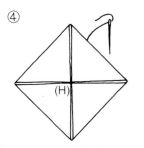

Join two more pieces in same manner to make block of four squares. Place window patches in place.

Navy with design

⑨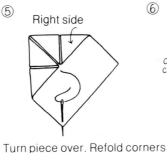

Fold edges of diamond over onto window patch as shown and slip-stitch.

⑩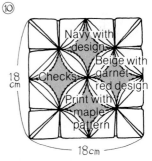

Make 66 blocks in same manner.

Navy with design

Beige with garnet-red design

18 cm

Checks

Print with maple pattern

18cm

51

53

52

Interior

DECORATE YOUR HOME

ASSORTED PILLOWS

Directions for 51 and 52 on page 84, for 53 on page 85, for 54 on page 86,
for 55 on page 88, for 56 on page 87, for 57 on page 88.

54

55

56

57

THOUSAND PYRAMIDS TABLECLOTH

Directions on page 90.

58

MOSAIC TABLE CENTER

Directions on page 91.

THOUSAND PYRAMIDS WALL HANGING

Directions on page 92.

61

OHIO STAR QUILT
Directions on page 93.

WALL POCKETS

Directions on page 94.

62

63

64
PILLOW CASE AND MATCHING BORDER FOR TOP SHEET
Directions on page 95.

SLIPPERS
Directions on page 97.

67

65

66

interior

FRAMED PATCHWORK PICTURES

Directions for 68 on page 96, for 69 on page 97, for 70 on page 99.

1—3　Appliquéd Pillows shown on page 1

MATERIALS: Cotton fabrics: for Pillow 1: gray, 80 cm by 44 cm; light turquoise, 30 cm by 20 cm; lavender, 23 cm by 12 cm; pink and olive, 18 cm square each; yellow, 16 cm by 8 cm; white, 12 cm square: for Pillow 2: ivory, 90 cm by 55 cm; yellow, 20 cm square; blue, 20 cm by 10 cm; turquoise and lavender, 13 cm by 10 cm each: for Pillow 3: light pink, 85 cm by 42 cm; turquoise, 28 cm by 15 cm; pink, 23 cm square; white, 22 cm by 15 cm; lavender, 17 cm by 13 cm; olive, 14 cm square; yellow and blue, 10 cm square each. For each pillow: #25 six-strand embroidery floss in white and colors to match appliqués; 31 cm long zipper; cotton fabric for inner pillow, 78 cm by 40 cm; kapok, 350 g.

FINISHED SIZE: 36 cm square

DIRECTIONS: 1. Cut out front pieces following Piecing Diagram. Place folded edge of second piece on seam line of first piece and stitch. Join pieces in this way to make front. 2. Enlarge appliqué patterns. Cut out appliqué pieces adding 0.7 cm seam allowance. Cut strips on the bias. Make a curve as shown with warm iron. Turn in raw edges of appliqué pieces and appliqué to front with two strands of embroidery floss in matching color. 3. Cut out two pieces for back. Sew zipper to back. With right sides of front and back together, stitch all around. Turn to right side. Insert inner pillow stuffed with kapok.

Appliqué Patterns

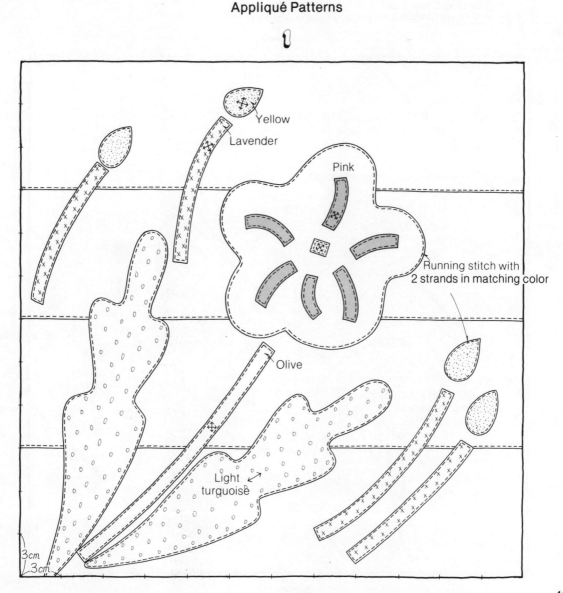

49

Diagram

Add 1 cm seam allowance.

Front   **Back**

Seam allowance

1   1

9   Gray

Join pieces

36

36

Gray   Zipper   2

1

18   18

2   Seam allowance   3   Seam allowance

1   1

12   Light pink

12

Ivory   Join pieces

8.5

Join pieces

36   36   36

Cut out back pieces for 2 and 3 from remaining fabrics
for front in same manner as for Pillow 1.

How to join pieces and appliqué

Turn in seam allowance
of appliqué piece.
Appliqué in place
using running stitch.

1cm

Turn in seam allowance and place on the first piece.
Sew pieces together in running stitch
with two strands of embroidery floss in white.

2

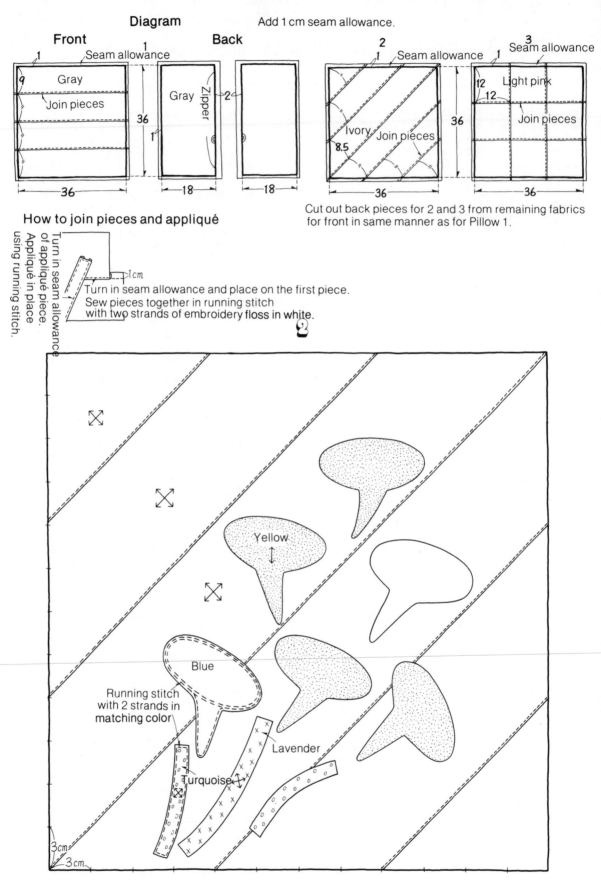

Yellow

Blue

Running stitch
with 2 strands in
matching color

Turquoise

Lavender

3cm

3cm

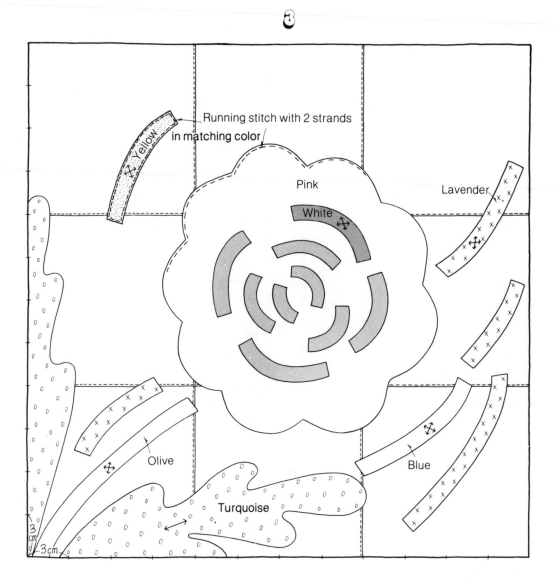

Running stitch with 2 strands
in matching color

Yellow

Pink

Lavender

White

Olive

Blue

Turquoise

3 cm

3 cm

4 Cosmetic Case with zipper shown on page 2

MATERIALS: Cotton fabrics: red, 90 cm by 15 cm; navy with gray floral design, 70 cm by 6 cm; emerald green, cream with leaf design, and ivory with red floral design, 48 cm by 6 cm each; dark pink with wine red floral design, red with floral design, gray with white floral design, 27 cm by 6 cm each; fabric for lining, 56 cm by 22 cm. 28.5 cm long zipper. Red bias binding tape, 1.2 cm by 170 cm.

FINISHED SIZE: See diagram.

DIRECTIONS: 1. Cut out pieces adding 0.7 cm seam allowance. Join four pieces together, placing cardboard shape on wrong side of each piece. 2. Cut out joining strips from red fabric. Assemble pieced blocks with red strips, following Piecing Diagram. 3. Join pieces for lining together with wrong sides facing. Tuck at each end of gusset. Sew end of zipper to gusset. With wrong sides of front and gusset together, bind raw edges using bias binding tape. Bind top edge and zipper with bias binding tape. Bind edges of back section in same manner.

Pattern
(Actual size)

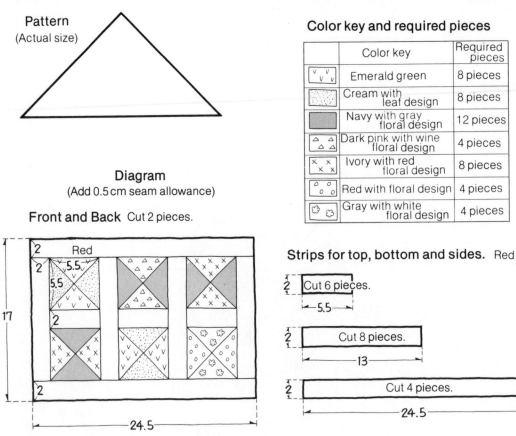

Color key and required pieces

	Color key	Required pieces
v v v	Emerald green	8 pieces
	Cream with leaf design	8 pieces
	Navy with gray floral design	12 pieces
△ △ △	Dark pink with wine floral design	4 pieces
x x x x	Ivory with red floral design	8 pieces
o o o	Red with floral design	4 pieces
	Gray with white floral design	4 pieces

Diagram
(Add 0.5 cm seam allowance)

Front and Back Cut 2 pieces.

2 Red
2
5.5
2
5.5
17
2
2
24.5

Cut out 2 pieces from lining fabric, 25.5 cm by 18 cm each.

Strips for top, bottom and sides. Red

2 Cut 6 pieces.
5.5

2 Cut 8 pieces.
13

2 Cut 4 pieces.
24.5

Gusset Cut 1 piece from red.

3
54.5

Cut out 1 piece for lining, 55.5 cm by 4 cm.

Finished diagram

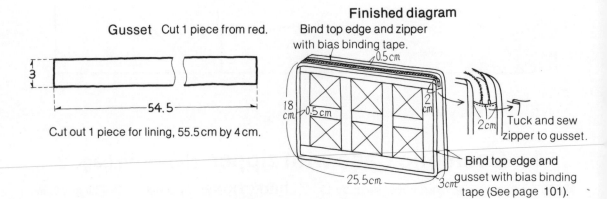

Bind top edge and zipper with bias binding tape.
0.5 cm
18 cm
0.5 cm
2 cm
25.5 cm
2 cm
3 cm
Tuck and sew zipper to gusset.
Bind top edge and gusset with bias binding tape (See page 101).

5   Cosmetic Case shown on page 2

MATERIALS: Cotton fabrics: pistachio green with white floral design, 50 cm by 24 cm; red with floral design, 40 cm by 17 cm; navy with gray floral design, 27 cm by 13 cm. Red bias binding tape, 1.2 cm by 78 cm.
FINISHED SIZE: See diagram.

DIRECTIONS: 1. Cut out patch pieces adding 0.7 cm seam allowance. Join pieces together by machine. 2. Fold raw edge of pocket opening twice and top-stitch. With wrong sides of front, lining and pocket together, bind raw edges with bias binding tape.

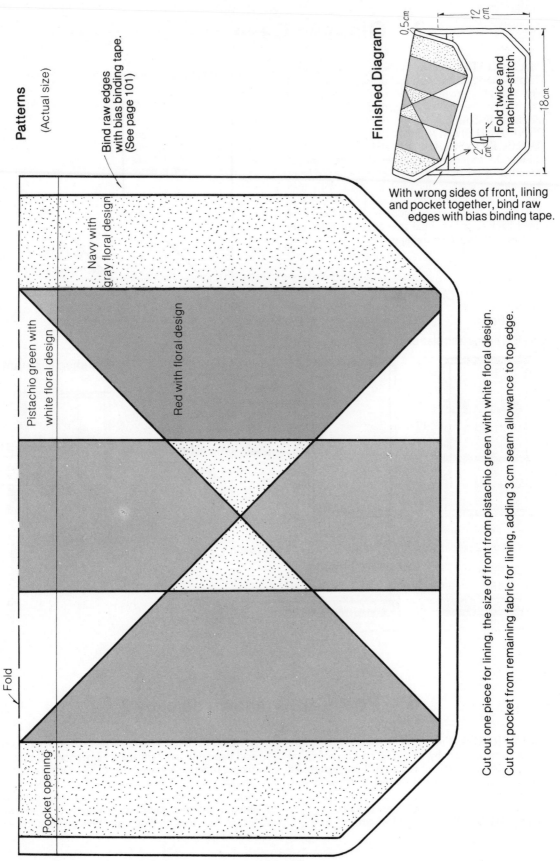

Patterns

(Actual size)

Bind raw edges with bias binding tape. (See page 101)

Navy with gray floral design

Pistachio green with white floral design

Red with floral design

Fold

Pocket opening

Finished Diagram

0.5 cm

12 cm

18 cm

2 cm

Fold twice and machine-stitch.

With wrong sides of front, lining and pocket together, bind raw edges with bias binding tape.

Cut out one piece for lining, the size of front from pistachio green with white floral design.

Cut out pocket from remaining fabric for lining, adding 3 cm seam allowance to top edge.

53

7 Glasses Case shown on page 3

MATERIALS: Cotton fabrics: emerald green, 35 cm square; cream with leaf design, 25 cm by 18 cm; pistachio green with white floral design, 20 cm by 9 cm; heavyweight cotton fabric for lining, 20 cm by 18 cm.

FINISHED SIZE: 10 cm by 17.5 cm

DIRECTIONS: 1. Cut out patch pieces for front adding 0.7 cm seam allowance. Join patch pieces together by machine. 2. With wrong sides of front and lining together, incase top edges with bias binding tape. Incase top edges of back in same manner. 3. With wrong sides of lined front and lined back together, bind raw edges of sides and bottom with bias binding tape.

Patterns (Actual size)

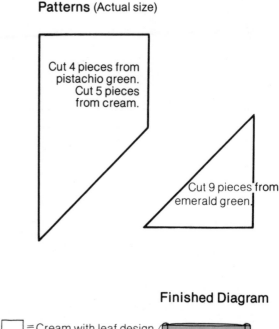

Cut 4 pieces from pistachio green.
Cut 5 pieces from cream.

Cut 9 pieces from emerald green.

Diagram

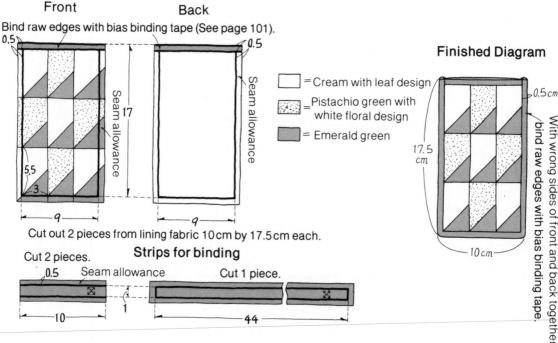

Front

Back

Bind raw edges with bias binding tape (See page 101).

= Cream with leaf design

= Pistachio green with white floral design

= Emerald green

Finished Diagram

With wrong sides of front and back together, bind raw edges with bias binding tape.

Cut out 2 pieces from lining fabric 10 cm by 17.5 cm each.

Strips for binding

Cut 2 pieces.

Seam allowance

Cut 1 piece.

---

6 Pen Case shown on page 2

MATERIALS: Cotton fabrics: gray with white floral design, 16 cm by 24 cm; ivory with red floral design, 30 cm by 10 cm; red with floral design, 20 cm by 7 cm; heavyweight cotton fabric for lining, 27 cm by 16 cm. Red bias binding tape, 1.2 cm by 60 cm. One pair of snap fasteners (small).

FINISHED SIZE: 7 cm by 18.5 cm

DIRECTIONS: 1. Cut out pieces for front, back and flap adding 0.7 cm seam allowance. Join patch pieces together by machine. 2. With right sides of pieced front and lining together, stitch along top edges. Turn to right side. With wrong sides of lined front and lined back together, bind raw edges with bias binding tape. Sew on snap fasteners in place.

Patterns (Actual size)

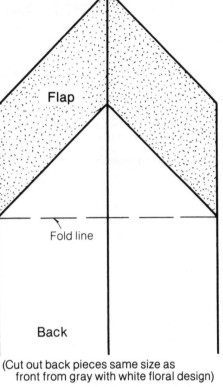

Flap

Fold line

Back

(Cut out back pieces same size as front from gray with white floral design)

Cut out lining for front, back and flap sam size as top pieces.

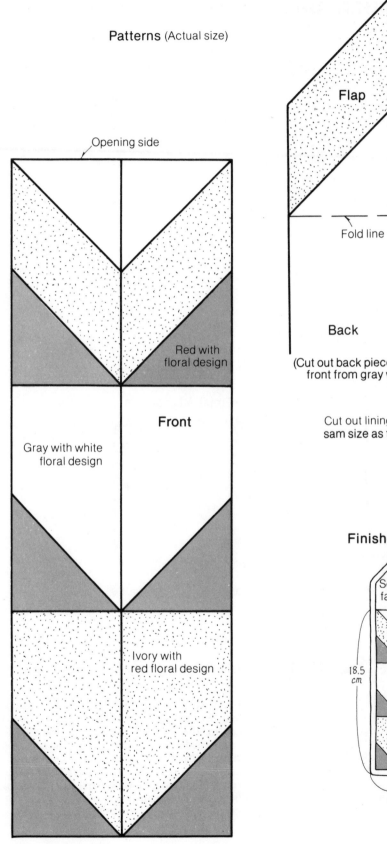

Opening side

Red with floral design

Front

Gray with white floral design

Ivory with red floral design

Finished Diagram

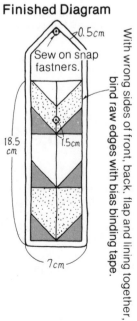

0.5cm

Sew on snap fastners.

18.5 cm

1.5cm

7cm

With wrong sides of front, back, flap and lining together, bind raw edges with bias binding tape.

9 Square Sachet shown on page 3

MATERIALS: Cotton fabrics: cream with leaf design, 18 cm by 12 cm; pink, 21 cm by 7 cm; scrap of apple green. White lace edging, 1.8 cm by 65 cm. Pink ribbon, 0.4 cm by 80 cm. Potpourri.

FINISHED SIZE: See diagram.

DIRECTIONS: 1. Cut out patch pieces for front adding 0.7 cm seam allowance. Overcast patch pieces together by hand, placing cardboard shape on wrong side of each piece. 2. With right sides of front and back together, stitch all around leaving opening for turning. Turn to right side. Insert potpourri. Slip-stitch opening closed. 3. Place gathered lace edging for ruffle all around. Stitch along center line of lace edging. Insert ribbon through lace and tie ribbon to bow at corners.

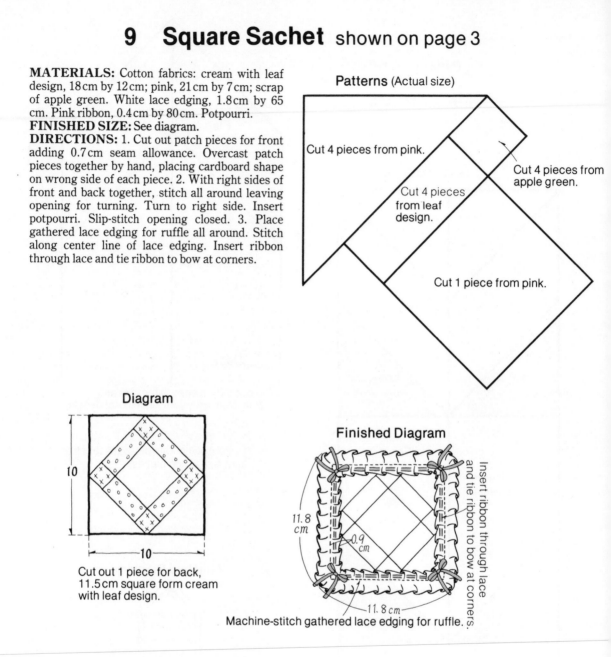

Patterns (Actual size)

Cut 4 pieces from pink.

Cut 4 pieces from apple green.

Cut 4 pieces from leaf design.

Cut 1 piece from pink.

Diagram

10

10

Cut out 1 piece for back, 11.5 cm square form cream with leaf design.

Finished Diagram

11.8 cm

0.9 cm

11.8 cm

Machine-stitch gathered lace edging for ruffle.

Insert ribbon through lace and tie ribbon to bow at corners.

8 Sachet shown on page 3

MATERIALS: Cotton fabrics: pink, 22 cm by 13 cm; cream with leaf design and ivory with red floral design, 13 cm by 7 cm each; pistachio green with white floral design, 11 cm by 6 cm. #25 six-strand embroidery floss in pink. White lace edging, 1.8 cm by 70 cm. Light pink ribbon, 0.6 cm by 50 cm. Potpourri.

FINISHED SIZE: See diagram.

DIRECTIONS: 1. Cut out patch pieces for front adding 0.7 cm seam allowance. Overcast patch pieces together by hand, placing cardboard shape on wrong side of each piece. 2. Attach ribbon carriers to front and back. With right sides of front and back together, stitch sides and bottom. 3. Turn to right side. Sew gathered lace edging for ruffle around top opening, sides and bottom. Insert ribbon through carriers and tie to bow.

Diagram

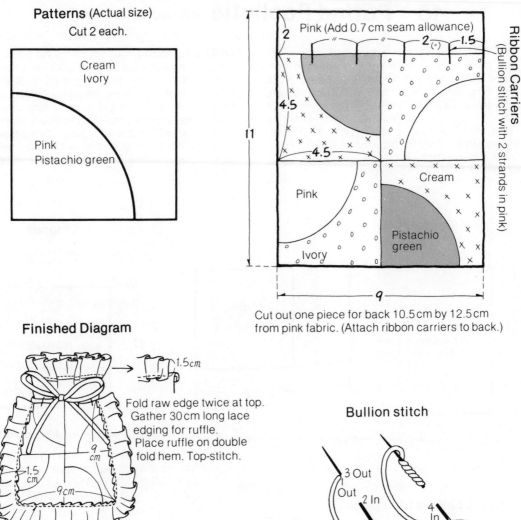

Patterns (Actual size)
Cut 2 each.

Cream
Ivory

Pink
Pistachio green

Pink (Add 0.7 cm seam allowance)

2

2

1.5

Ribbon Carriers
(Bullion stitch with 2 strands in pink)

11

4.5

4.5

Pink

Ivory

Cream

Pistachio
green

9

Cut out one piece for back 10.5 cm by 12.5 cm
from pink fabric. (Attach ribbon carriers to back.)

Finished Diagram

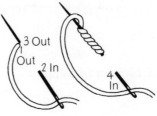

1.5 cm

Fold raw edge twice at top.
Gather 30 cm long lace
edging for ruffle.
Place ruffle on double
fold hem. Top-stitch.

9 cm

1.5 cm

9 cm

Gather 40 cm long lace edging for ruffle.
Stitch ruffle to front.

Bullion stitch

3 Out

Out

2 In

4 In

10   Puffed Pochette shown on page 4

MATERIALS: Cotton fabrics: red with white dots, green with white dots, pink with white dots, bright yellow with floral design, yellow, balck with floral design, blue, navy with floral design, dark pink, 16cm by 8cm each; back pieces for puffs, 54cm by 12cm; fabric for lining, 26cm by 13cm. Red bias binding tape, 1.2cm by 212cm. White button, 2cm in diameter. Adhesive interlining, 1cm by 70cm. Polyester fiberfill.
FINISHED SIZE: See diagram.

DIRECTIONS: 1. Cut out pieces for puffs. Following directions for making puff on page 19, make puffs and sew them together. 2. Bind top edges of front and lining with bias binding tape. Bind top edges of back and lining in same manner. With wrong sides of lined front and back together, bind sides and bottom with bias binding tape. 3. Make handle and loop for button with bias binding tape. Attach handle and loop in place. Sew on button.

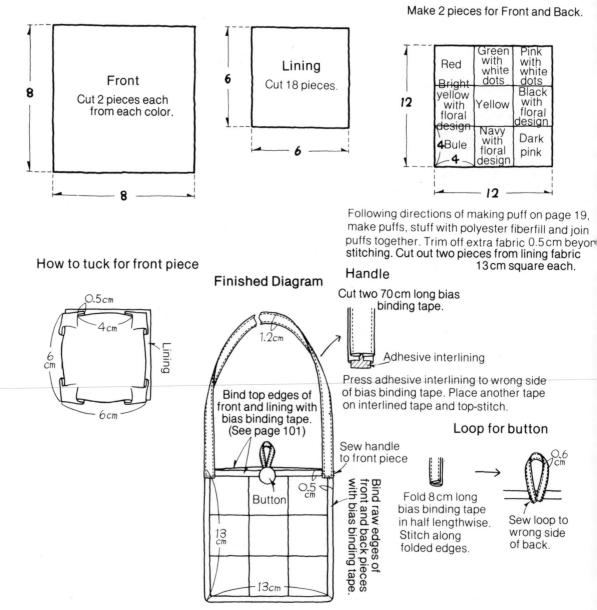

Size for Puff

Front
Cut 2 pieces each from each color.
8 × 8

Lining
Cut 18 pieces.
6 × 6

Diagram

Make 2 pieces for Front and Back.

Red	Green with white dots	Pink with white dots
Bright yellow with floral design	Yellow	Black with floral design
Bule	Navy with floral design	Dark pink

12 × 12 · 4 · 4

Following directions of making puff on page 19, make puffs, stuff with polyester fiberfill and join puffs together. Trim off extra fabric 0.5cm beyond stitching. Cut out two pieces from lining fabric 13cm square each.

How to tuck for front piece

0.5cm · 4cm · 6cm · 6cm · Lining

Finished Diagram

1.2cm
Bind top edges of front and lining with bias binding tape. (See page 101)
Button
0.5 cm
13 cm
13cm
Bind raw edges of front and back pieces with bias binding tape.

Handle

Cut two 70cm long bias binding tape.

Adhesive interlining

Press adhesive interlining to wrong side of bias binding tape. Place another tape on interlined tape and top-stitch.

Sew handle to front piece

Loop for button

0.6 cm
Fold 8cm long bias binding tape in half lengthwise. Stitch along folded edges.
Sew loop to wrong side of back.

11 Pochette shown on page 4

MATERIALS: Cotton fabrics: yellow with floral design, 30 cm by 20 cm; green, 25 cm by 7 cm; orange, 17 cm by 9 cm; red with floral design, 14 cm by 7 cm; brown with floral design, 7 cm square; fabric for lining, 33 cm by 16 cm. #30 white cotton thread. Quilt batting, 17 cm square. Brown cotton cord, 0.5 cm in diameter and 87 cm long. Green button, 2 cm in diameter.
FINISHED SIZE: See diagram.

DIRECTIONS: 1. Cut out patch pieces for front adding 0.7 cm seam allowance. Sew patch pieces together by hand. 2. Pin and baste pieced top, batting and lining together. Quilt as indicated. 3. Place back section on lining with wrong sides together. With right sides of front and back together, stitch sides and bottom. 4. Turn in raw edges at top and slip-stitch to wrong side. Sew handle and loop for button in place. Sew on button.

Patterns (Actual size)

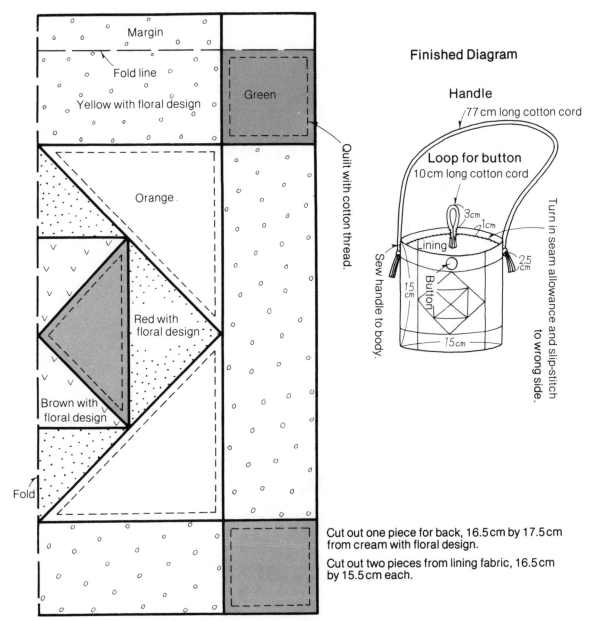

Finished Diagram

Handle
77 cm long cotton cord

Loop for button
10 cm long cotton cord

Cut out one piece for back, 16.5 cm by 17.5 cm from cream with floral design.

Cut out two pieces from lining fabric, 16.5 cm by 15.5 cm each.

12 Girl Tote Bag shown on page 4

MATERIALS: Green denim, 49cm by 93cm. Unbleached canvas, 23cm by 31cm. Cotton fabrics: yellow with floral design, 36cm by 6cm; brown with white checks, 13cm by 10cm; white, 12cm by 8cm; black with red floral design, black with orange floral design, 15cm by 5cm; white with floral design, brown with floral design, red with floral design, 10cm by 5cm each; brown, 8cm by 6cm; fabric for lining, 37cm by 73cm. #25 six-strand embroidery floss in gray-brown, black, pink and wine red.

FINISHED SIZE: See diagram.
DIRECTIONS: 1. Cut out patch pieces adding 0.7cm seam allowance. Sew patch pieces for skirt together by hand. 2. Braid hair and insert top of braid between hair and brim. Slip-stitch appliqués to panel. 3. Stitch appliquéd panel in place. Turn in top edge of front and sew handle in place. 4. Stitch each side of outer bag. Make inner bag. With wrong sides of outer and inner bags together, slip-stitch folded edge to outer bag around top.

Diagram

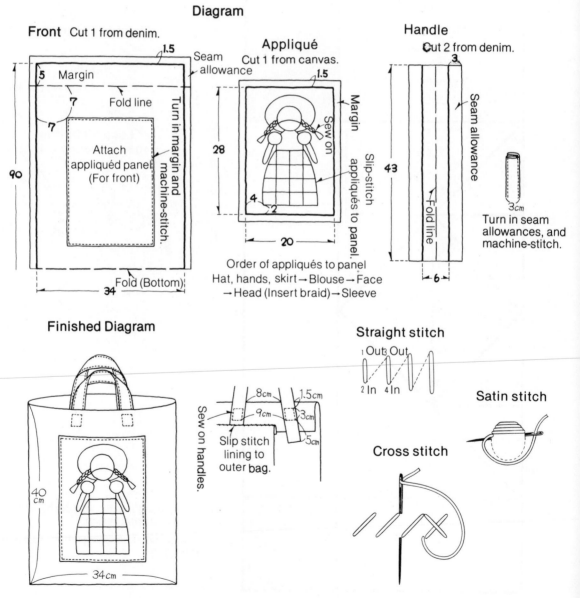

Front Cut 1 from denim.

Seam allowance

1.5

5 Margin

Fold line

7

7

Attach appliquéd panel (For front)

Turn in margin and machine-stitch.

90

34

Fold (Bottom)

Appliqué Cut 1 from canvas.

1.5

Margin

Sew on

28

4

2

20

Slip-stitch appliqués to panel.

Order of appliqués to panel
Hat, hands, skirt → Blouse → Face → Head (Insert braid) → Sleeve

Handle Cut 2 from denim.

3

Seam allowance

43

Fold line

6

3cm

Turn in seam allowances, and machine-stitch.

Finished Diagram

Sew on handles.

8cm

9cm

1.5cm

3cm

5cm

Slip stitch lining to outer bag.

40 cm

34 cm

Straight stitch

Out Out

In In

Satin stitch

Cross stitch

60

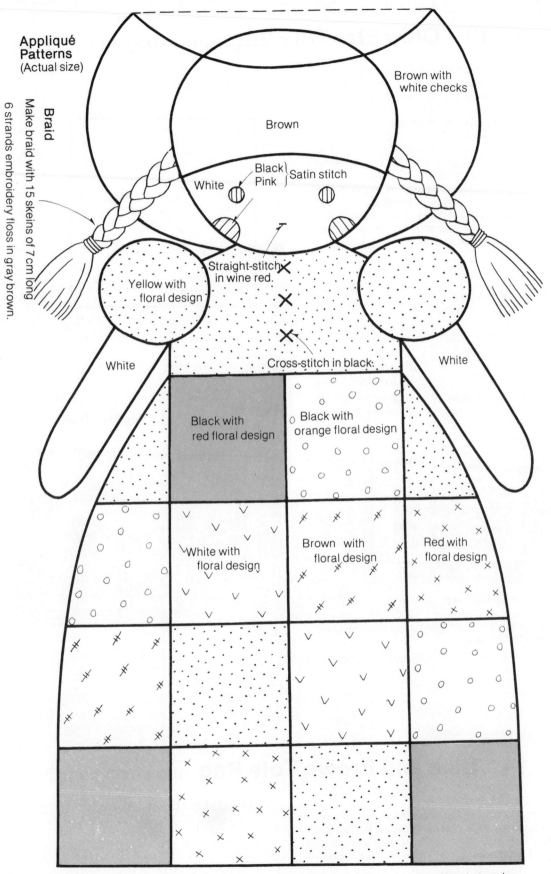

Appliqué Patterns
(Actual size)

Braid
Make braid with 15 skeins of 7 cm long
6 strands embroidery floss in gray brown.

Brown with
white checks

Brown

White

Black
Pink

Satin stitch

Straight-stitch
in wine red.

Yellow with
floral design

White

White

Cross-stitch in black:

Black with
red floral design

Black with
orange floral design

White with
floral design

Brown with
floral design

Red with
floral design

Use 4 strands.

61

13 Ohio Star Tote Bag shown on page 4

MATERIALS: Unbleached canvas, 90 cm by 49 cm. Cotton fabrics: pink, 86 cm by 25 cm; white print, 72 cm by 23 cm; pink print, 14 cm by 7 cm; fabric for lining, 61 cm by 45 cm.

FINISHED SIZE: See diagram.

DIRECTIONS: 1. Cut out patch pieces adding 0.7 cm seam allowance. Sew patch pieces together by hand. 2. Sew strips for border to canvas, with right sides together and 0.7 cm seams. 3. Slip-stitch pieced blocks to canvas in place. 4. With right sides of front and back together, stitch sides and bottom. Make inner bag. Insert inner bag and slip-stitch to outer bag, with handles in between. Machine-stitch handles to bag.

Pattern (Actual size)

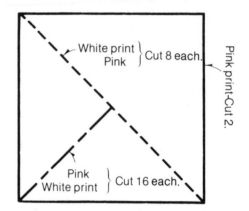

White print
Pink } Cut 8 each.

Pink print-Cut 2.

Pink
White print } Cut 16 each.

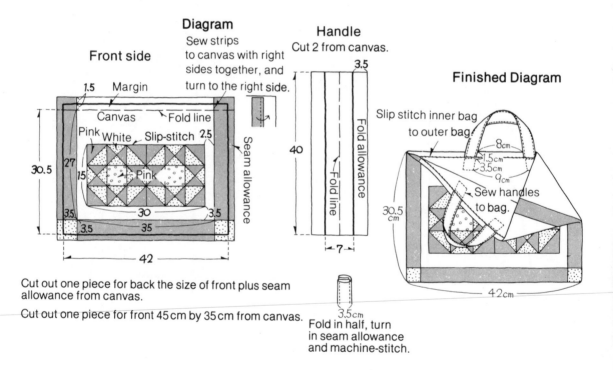

Diagram

Sew strips to canvas with right sides together, and turn to the right side.

Front side

1.5 Margin

Canvas   Fold line

Pink White   Slip-stitch 2.5

Pink

Seam allowance

30.5

27

15

30

3.5   3.5

3.5   35

42

Cut out one piece for back the size of front plus seam allowance from canvas.

Cut out one piece for front 45 cm by 35 cm from canvas.

Handle
Cut 2 from canvas.

3.5

40

Fold allowance

Fold line

Fold allowance

7

3.5 cm

Fold in half, turn in seam allowance and machine-stitch.

Finished Diagram

Slip stitch inner bag to outer bag

8 cm
1.5 cm
3.5 cm
9 cm

Sew handles to bag.

30.5 cm

42 cm

14 Blue and Brown Tote Bag shown on page 5

MATERIALS: Cotton fabrics: blue-gray, 90 cm by 46 cm; dark brown, 28 cm by 24 cm; 30 pieces of 8 cm by 6 cm (see photo for colors and designs); fabric for lining, 62 cm by 38 cm. #40 white cotton thread. 4-ply yarn. Quilt batting, 74 cm by 35 cm.

FINISHED SIZE: See diagram.

DIRECTIONS: 1. Cut out patch pieces for hexagons adding 0.7cm seam allowance. Sew six triangles together by hand to make hexagon. Make five hexagons. 2. Cut out rectangles adding 1cm seam allowance. Slip-stitch hexagon to each blue-gray rectangle, matching centers. Join appliquéd blue-gray rectangles and dark brown rectangles together. 3. Place pieced front on batting. Quilt along quilting lines. Quilt on back section in same manner. With right sides of front and back together, stitch sides, bottom and corners. 4. Place battig on wrong side of strip for top border and quilt. Stitch ends of strip to make a circle. Make inner bag. With wrong sides of outer and inner bags together, run a gathering stitch. Pull thread to fit joined strip. Place joined strip on gathered front and stitch. Fold joined strip in half lengthwise and slip-stitch to lining. 5. Make handles and insert 4-ply yarn. Attach handles in place.

Patterns

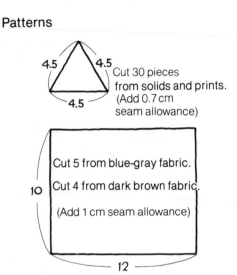

4.5   4.5

4.5

Cut 30 pieces from solids and prints. (Add 0.7cm seam allowance)

Cut 5 from blue-gray fabric.
Cut 4 from dark brown fabric.
(Add 1 cm seam allowance)

10

12

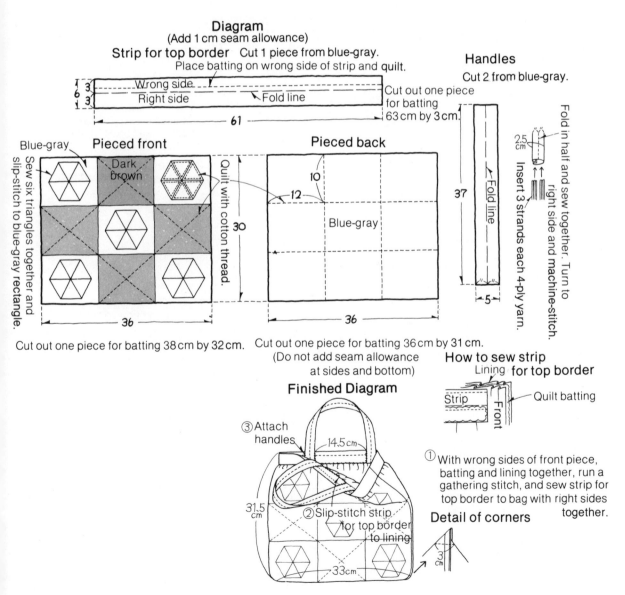

Diagram
(Add 1 cm seam allowance)
Strip for top border   Cut 1 piece from blue-gray.
Place batting on wrong side of strip and quilt.

Wrong side
Right side   ←Fold line
Cut out one piece for batting 63 cm by 3 cm.
61
1 3 6 3 1

Handles
Cut 2 from blue-gray.

Fold line
37
5
2.5 cm

Fold in half and sew together. Turn to right side and machine-stitch.
Insert 3 strands each 4-ply yarn.

Pieced front
Blue-gray
Dark brown
Sew six triangles together and slip-stitch to blue-gray rectangle.
Quilt with cotton thread.
30
36
Cut out one piece for batting 38 cm by 32 cm.

Pieced back
10
12
Blue-gray
36
Cut out one piece for batting 36 cm by 31 cm.
(Do not add seam allowance at sides and bottom)

Finished Diagram
③Attach handles   14.5 cm
31.5 cm
②Slip-stitch strip for top border to lining
33 cm

How to sew strip for top border
Lining
Strip   Front
Quilt batting

① With wrong sides of front piece, batting and lining together, run a gathering stitch, and sew strip for top border to bag with right sides together.

Detail of corners
3 cm

15 Striped Tote Bag shown on page 5

MATERIALS: Cotton fabrics: (see list for colors and amounts) fabric for lining, 76cm by 48cm. #40 white cotton thread. Quilt batting, 76cm by 64cm.
FINISHED SIZE: See diagram.
DIRECTIONS: 1. Cut out patch pieces adding seam allowance. Join patch pieces together by machine. Trim off extra fabric 1cm beyond stitching at each side and bottom. 2. Make another piece for back in same manner. Place pieced top on batting and quilt. With right sides of quilted front and back together, stitch sides and bottom. 3. Make inner bag. Insert inner bag. Bind top edges of outer and inner bags with binding strip. 4. Braid stuffed strips for handle. Attach handles in place.

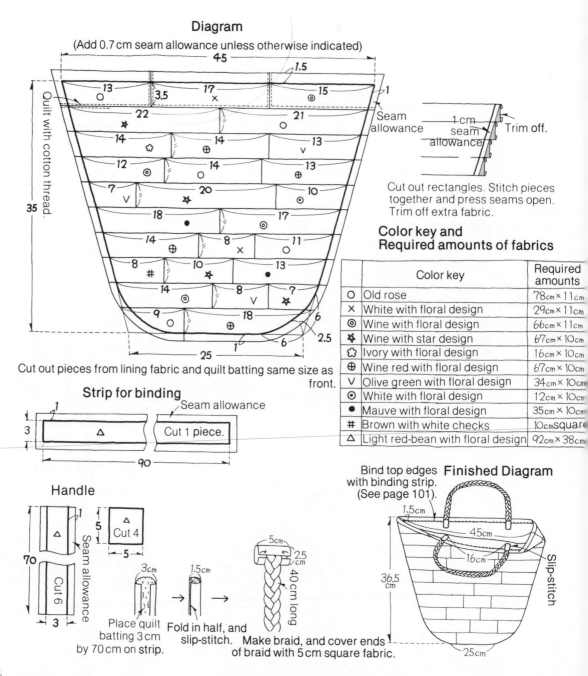

Diagram
(Add 0.7 cm seam allowance unless otherwise indicated)

Cut out rectangles. Stitch pieces together and press seams open. Trim off extra fabric.

Cut out pieces from lining fabric and quilt batting same size as front.

Strip for binding

Cut 1 piece.

Handle

Cut 4
Cut 6

Place quilt batting 3cm by 70cm on strip.
Fold in half, and slip-stitch.
Make braid, and cover ends of braid with 5cm square fabric.

Bind top edges with binding strip. (See page 101).

Finished Diagram

Slip-stitch

Color key and Required amounts of fabrics

	Color key	Required amounts
O	Old rose	78cm × 11cm
×	White with floral design	29cm × 11cm
◎	Wine with floral design	66cm × 11cm
✻	Wine with star design	67cm × 10cm
✿	Ivory with floral design	16cm × 10cm
⊕	Wine red with floral design	67cm × 10cm
V	Olive green with floral design	34cm × 10cm
⊙	White with floral design	12cm × 10cm
●	Mauve with floral design	35cm × 10cm
#	Brown with white checks	10cm square
△	Light red-bean with floral design	92cm × 38cm

16 Satin Pochette shown on page 5

MATERIALS: Lightweight satin: pale blue, 48 cm by 23 cm; pink and lavender, 17 cm by 8 cm each. Cotton print, 17 cm by 23 cm. Silver metallic thread. #50 white cotton thread. Quilt batting, 34 cm by 23 cm. Blue bias binding tape, 1.8 cm by 185 cm. Cotton cord, 0.5 cm in diameter and 117 cm long. Four heart-shaped buttons, 1 cm in diameter. One pair of snap fasteners (large).
FINISHED SIZE: See diagram.

DIRECTIONS: 1. Cut out patch pieces for front adding seam allowance. Sew patch pieces together by hand. 2. Insert batting between pieced front and lining. Quilt along quilting lines with silver metallic thread. Quilt on back through all thicknesses with cotton sewing thread. 3. With wrong sides of front and back together, bind raw edges with bias binding tape. Make handle and sew it in place. Sew on buttons and snap fasteners in place.

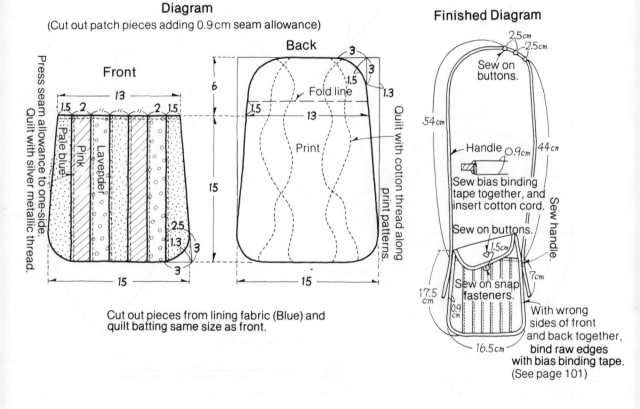

Diagram
(Cut out patch pieces adding 0.9 cm seam allowance)

Finished Diagram

Cut out pieces from lining fabric (Blue) and quilt batting same size as front.

17 Tray Mat shown on page 6

MATERIALS: Cotton fabrics: blue, 90 cm by 50 cm; beige with floral design, 66 cm by 20 cm; beige, 55 cm by 45 cm; pink, 26 cm by 13 cm. #25 six-strand embroidery floss in beige. Quilt batting, 37 cm square.
FINISHED SIZE: 37 cm in diameter

DIRECTIONS: 1. Cut out patch pieces adding 0.7 cm seam allowance. Overcast patch pieces together by hand, placing cardboard shape on wrong side of each piece. 2. Insert batting between pieced top and lining and quilt as indicated. Bind raw edges with bias binding tape.

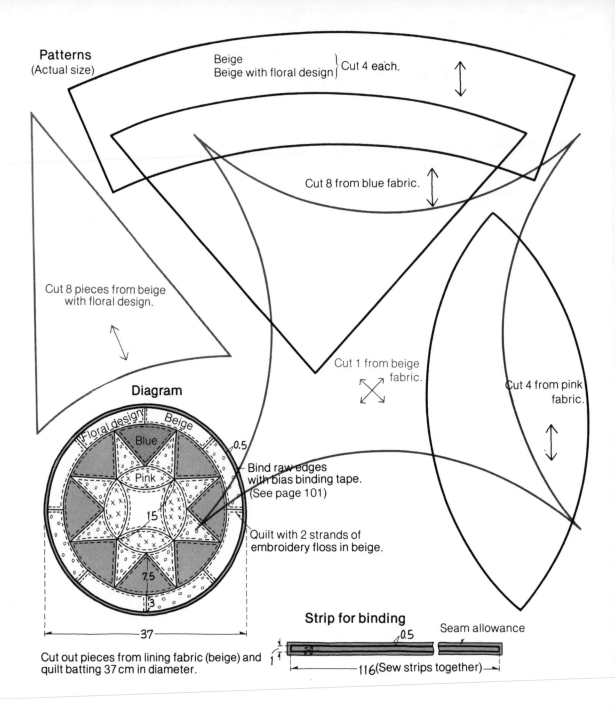

Patterns
(Actual size)

Beige
Beige with floral design } Cut 4 each.

Cut 8 from blue fabric.

Cut 8 pieces from beige with floral design.

Cut 1 from beige fabric.

Cut 4 from pink fabric.

Diagram

Floral design
Beige
Blue
Pink
0.5
15
7.5
3
37

Bind raw edges with bias binding tape. (See page 101)

Quilt with 2 strands of embroidery floss in beige.

Cut out pieces from lining fabric (beige) and quilt batting 37 cm in diameter.

Strip for binding

0.5
Seam allowance
1
116 (Sew strips together)

18 Hot Mitt shown on page 6

MATERIALS: Cotton fabrics: lavender, 58 cm by 20 cm; cream with floral design, 29 cm by 12 cm; lavender with white stripes, 18 cm by 8.5 cm; lavender with white checks, 10 cm by 4 cm; fabric for lining, 40 cm by 27 cm. #25 six-strand embroidery floss in lavender. Quilt batting, 40 cm by 27 cm. Lavender bias binding tape, 1.2 cm by 81 cm.
FINISHED SIZE: See diagram.

DIRECTIONS: 1. Cut out patch pieces adding 0.7 cm seam allowance. Join patch pieces together by machine. 2. With right sides of pieced top and lining together, stitch along wrist edge. Turn to right side. Stitch wrist edges of back piece and lining in same manner. Insert batting between top and lining. Quilt as indicated. 3. With wrong sides of two pieces together, and loop for hanging in between, bind raw edges with bias binding tape.

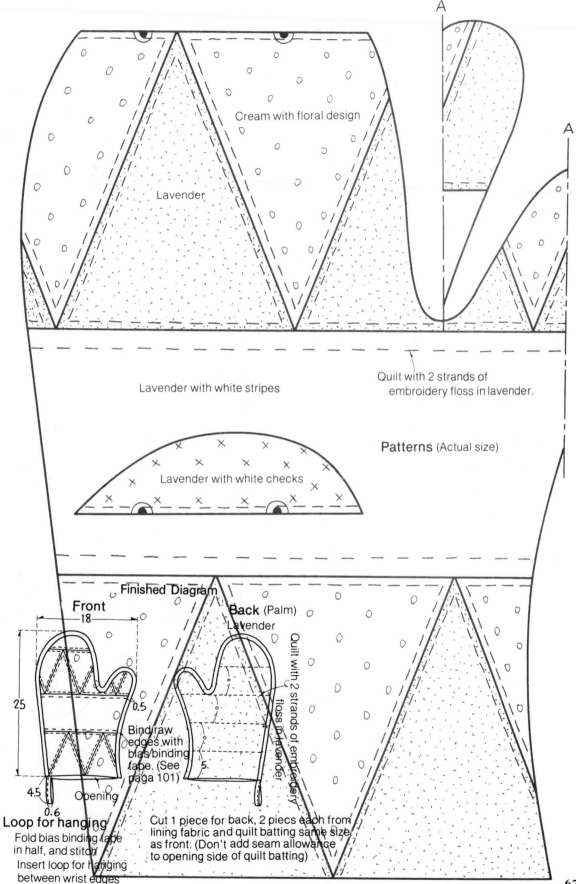

A

A

Cream with floral design

Lavender

Quilt with 2 strands of embroidery floss in lavender.

Lavender with white stripes

Lavender with white checks

Patterns (Actual size)

Finished Diagram

Front
18

25

0.5

Bind raw edges with bias/binding tape. (See page 101)

4.5

Opening

0.6

Loop for hanging
Fold bias binding tape in half, and stitch
Insert loop for hanging between wrist edges

Back (Palm)
Lavender

5

Quilt with 2 strands of embroidery floss in lavender

Cut 1 piece for back, 2 piecs each from lining fabric and quilt batting same size as front: (Don't add seam allowance to opening side of quilt batting)

67

19 Handle Cover shown on page 6

MATERIALS: Cotton fabrics: mauve with floral design, 46 cm by 8 cm; dark mauve and beige with white floral design, 20 cm by 8 cm each; fabric for lining, 18 cm by 13 cm. #25 six-strand embroidery floss in light brown. Quilt batting, 18 cm by 13 cm. Lavender bias binding tape, 1.2 cm by 50 cm.

FINISHED SIZE: See diagram.

DIRECTIONS: Make Handle Cover in same manner as for 18. Mitt. Quilt along quilting lines on back. Attach loop for hanging to top of Cover.

Loop for hanging

0.6 cm

→

Fold 11 cm long binding tape in half lengthwise, turn in seam allowances and stitch.

↓

Turn in seams and stitch.

Back (Mauve with floral design)
Lining (2 pieces)
Quilt batting (2 pieces) } Cut out pieces same size as front.

Diagram

(Actual size)

5

Beige with white floral design

0.5

Mauve with floral design

Quilting line on back

Dark mauve

Quilt with 2 strands of embroidery floss in light brown.

Bind raw edges with bias binding tape. (See page 101)

16.5

Opening

6

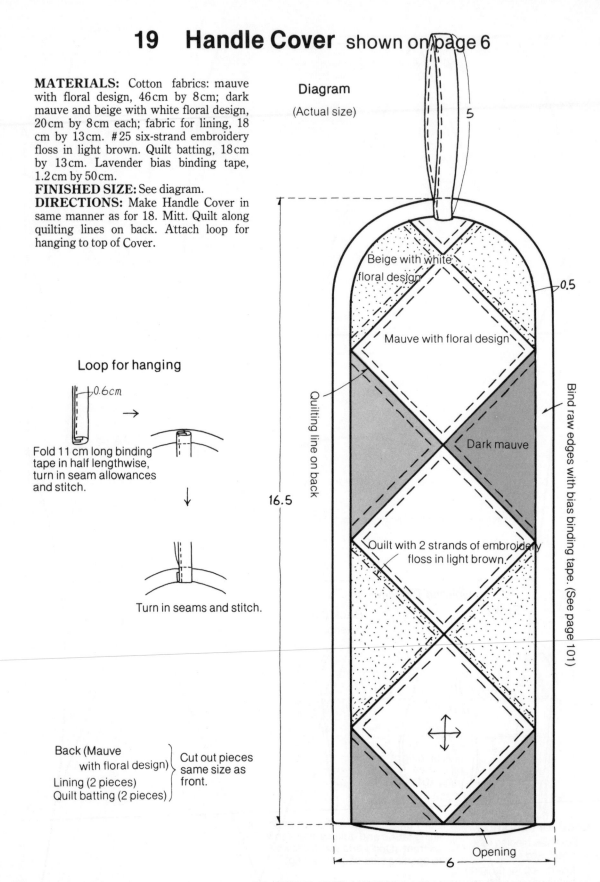

20 Square Potholder shown on page 6

MATERIALS: Cotton fabrics; mauve with floral design, 40 cm by 22 cm; cream with floral design, 21 cm by 18 cm; light mauve, 22 cm by 19 cm. Silk sewing thread in lavender. Quilt batting, 22 cm square. Lavender bias binding tape, 1.2 cm by 91 cm.
FINISHED SIZE: 21.5 cm square.

DIRECTIONS: 1. Cut out patch pieces adding 0.7 cm seam allowance. Join patch pieces together by machine. 2. Place batting on lining. Place pieced top on batting. Quilt along quilting lines using double strands of silk sewing thread in lavender. Bind raw edges with bias binding tape. Attach loop for handging.

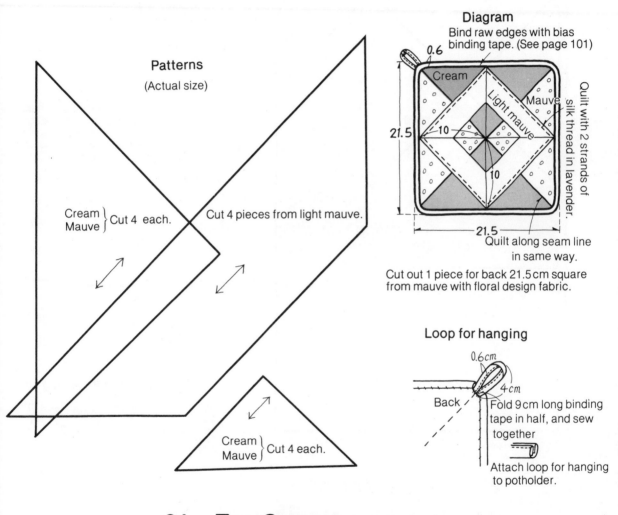

Patterns
(Actual size)

Cream
Mauve } Cut 4 each.

Cut 4 pieces from light mauve.

Cream
Mauve } Cut 4 each.

Diagram
Bind raw edges with bias binding tape. (See page 101)

0.6

Cream

Light mauve

Mauve

21.5

10

10

Quilt with 2 strands of silk thread in lavender.

21.5

Quilt along seam line in same way.

Cut out 1 piece for back 21.5 cm square from mauve with floral design fabric.

Loop for hanging

0.6 cm

4 cm

Back

Fold 9 cm long binding tape in half, and sew together

Attach loop for hanging to potholder.

21 Tea Cozy shown on page 7

MATERIALS: Cotton fabrics: pink, 88 cm by 16 cm; gray with floral design, 76 cm by 14 cm; pink with floral design, 75 cm by 11 cm; light pink, 47 cm by 21 cm; fabric for lining, 72 cm by 27 cm. Polyester fiberfill.
FINISHED SIZE: See diagram.

DIRCTIONS: 1. Cut out patch pieces adding 1 cm seam allowance. Join patch pieces together by machine. 2. With right sides of two pieces together and loop for hanging in between, stitch all around leaving bottom open. Turn to right side. 3. Make lining in same manner. Place polyester fiberfill all over lining piece. 4. Place pieced top over polyester fiberfill. Turn in seam allowance of lining and slip-stitch in place.

69

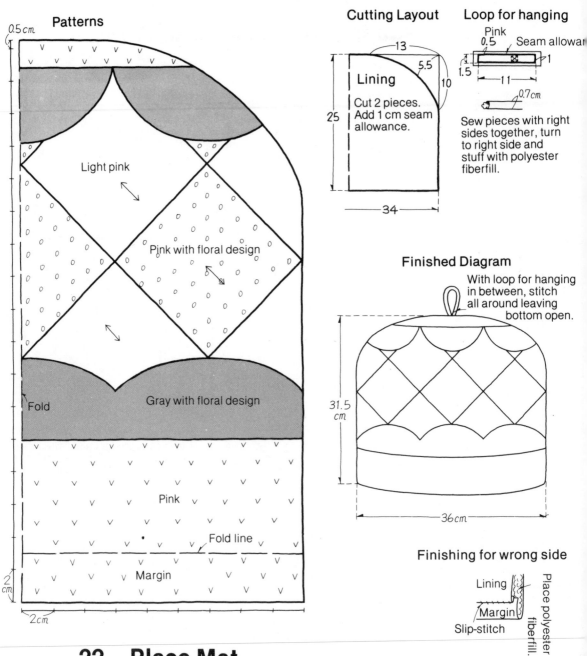

Patterns

0.5 cm

V V V V V V V

Light pink

Pink with floral design

Fold

Gray with floral design

V V V V V V V V

V V V V V V V

V V V V V V V

V V V V V V V

V V V V V V V

Pink

V V V V V V V

Fold line

V V V V V V V

V V V V V V V

Margin

V V V V V V V

2 cm

2 cm

Cutting Layout

13

5.5

10

Lining

Cut 2 pieces.
Add 1 cm seam
allowance.

25

34

Loop for hanging

Pink
0.5

Seam allowance

1.5

1

11

0.7 cm

Sew pieces with right
sides together, turn
to right side and
stuff with polyester
fiberfill.

Finished Diagram

With loop for hanging
in between, stitch
all around leaving
bottom open.

31.5
cm

36 cm

Finishing for wrong side

Lining

Margin

Slip-stitch

Place polyester
fiberfill.

22   Place Mat
23   Matching Napkin shown on page 7

MATERIALS: For 22: cotton fabrics: pink, 38 cm by 29 cm; gray with floral design, 90 cm by 21 cm; green with white checks, 10 cm square; gray, 26 cm by 6 cm; dark pink, 20 cm by 10 cm; light gray-green, 18 cm by 10 cm; fabric for lining, 38 cm by 29 cm. #25 six-strand embroidery floss in pink. For 23: cotton fabrics: pink, 42 cm square; gray with floral design, 32 cm by 5 cm; green with white checks, 9 cm square.
FINISHED SIZE: 22: 42 cm by 32.5 cm. 23: 40 cm square.

DIRECTIONS: For 22: 1. Cut out appliqué pieces adding 0.7 cm seam allowance. Overcast appliqué pieces together by hand, placing cardboard shape on wrong side of each piece. Slip-stitch pieced appliqués to background fabric. 2. Place appliquéd piece on lining with wrong sides together. Stitch in running stitch as indicated. Sew strips for border all around.

Patterns (Actual size)

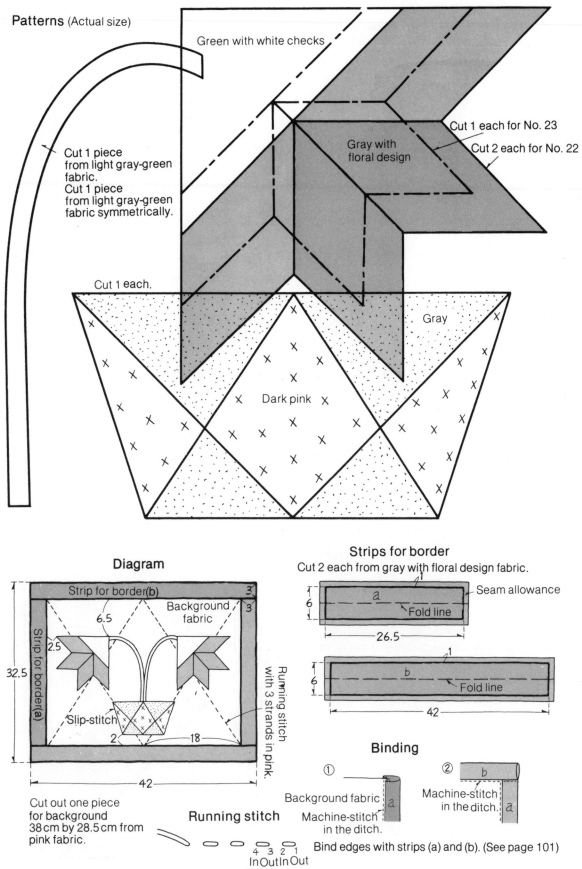

Green with white checks

Cut 1 piece
from light gray-green
fabric.
Cut 1 piece
from light gray-green
fabric symmetrically.

Gray with
floral design

Cut 1 each for No. 23

Cut 2 each for No. 22

Cut 1 each.

Gray

Dark pink

Diagram

Strip for border (b)

Background
fabric

Strip for border (a)

6.5

2.5

32.5

Slip-stitch

Running stitch
with 3 strands in pink.

2

18

42

Cut out one piece
for background
38 cm by 28.5 cm from
pink fabric.

Running stitch

4 3 2 1
In Out In Out

Strips for border

Cut 2 each from gray with floral design fabric.

a

Seam allowance

Fold line

6

26.5

b

Fold line

6

42

Binding

① Background fabric

a

Machine-stitch
in the ditch.

② b

Machine-stitch
in the ditch.

a

Bind edges with strips (a) and (b). (See page 101)

For 23: 1. Join appliqué pieces in same manner as for Place Mat. 2. Make double hem and top-stitch.

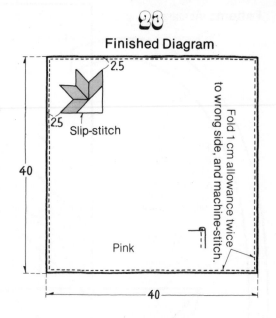

23
Finished Diagram

2.5

2.5
Slip-stitch

Fold 1 cm allowance twice to wrong side, and machine-stitch.

40

Pink

40

28　Bird Pillow shown on page 21

MATERIALS: Cotton fabrics: grayish wine red, 60 cm by 37 cm; pink, 90 cm by 30 cm; rosepink with pink floral design, 90 cm by 24 cm; blue-gray and gray-brown, 45 cm by 10 cm each; gray with floral design, 45 cm by 8 cm; pink with rosepink floral design, ivory with floral design, 23 cm by 8 cm each; pistachio green and yellow-brown, 21 cm by 10 cm each; mustard, 17 cm by 15 cm. #25 six-strand embroidery floss in navy and colors to match appliqués. 30 cm long zipper. Cotton fabric for inner pillow, 76 cm by 39 cm. Kapok, 350 g.
FINISHED SIZE: 35 cm square (except ruffle)
DIRECTIONS: 1. Cut out patch pieces for front adding 0.7 cm seam allowance. Overcast patch pieces together by hand, placing cardboard shape on wrong side of each piece. 2. Enlarge appliqué patterns. Cut out appliqué pieces adding 0.7 cm seam allowance. Sew appliqué pieces together in same manner as for ptach pieces. 3 and 4. Make up for pillow as for 27.

Pattern (Actual size)

Cut 6 pieces each from e and f.

Cut 3 pieces each from g and h.

Cut 9 pieces each from a, b, c and d.

Diagram
Front

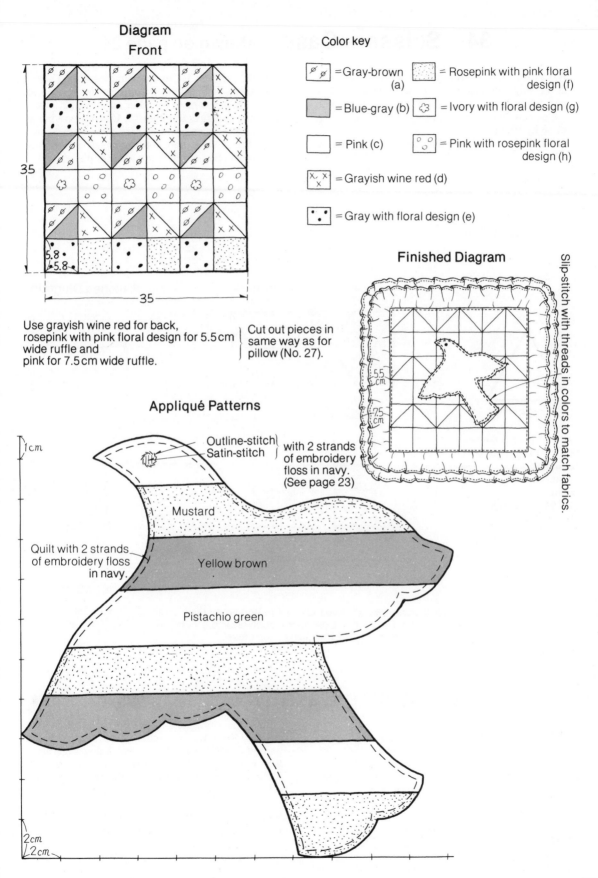

35

35

5.8
5.8

Use grayish wine red for back,
rosepink with pink floral design for 5.5 cm
wide ruffle and
pink for 7.5 cm wide ruffle.

Cut out pieces in
same way as for
pillow (No. 27).

Color key

☒ = Gray-brown (a)

⬜ = Blue-gray (b)

⬜ = Pink (c)

☒ = Grayish wine red (d)

⬜ = Gray with floral design (e)

⬜ = Rosepink with pink floral design (f)

⬜ = Ivory with floral design (g)

⬜ = Pink with rosepink floral design (h)

Finished Diagram

Slip-stitch with threads in colors to match fabrics.

5.5 cm

7.5 cm

Appliqué Patterns

1 cm

Outline-stitch
Satin-stitch
with 2 strands
of embroidery
floss in navy.
(See page 23)

Mustard

Quilt with 2 strands
of embroidery floss
in navy.

Yellow brown

Pistachio green

2 cm
2 cm

34 Scissors Case shown on page 24

MATERIALS: Cotton fabrics: brown, 23 cm by 12 cm; white with light brown floral design, yellow with white floral design, light yellow-green with leaf design, 20 cm by 12 cm each; fabric for lining, 23 cm by 16 cm.
FINISHED SIZE: See diagram.

DIRECTIONS: 1. Cut out triangles adding seam allowance. Sew triangles together in horizontal rows. Then sew rows together as shown. 2. Overcast bottom edges together. 3. Cut out one piece for lining the size of outer case plus seam allowance. Stitch sides and bottom. Insert lining into outer piece. Slip-stitch lining to outer piece.

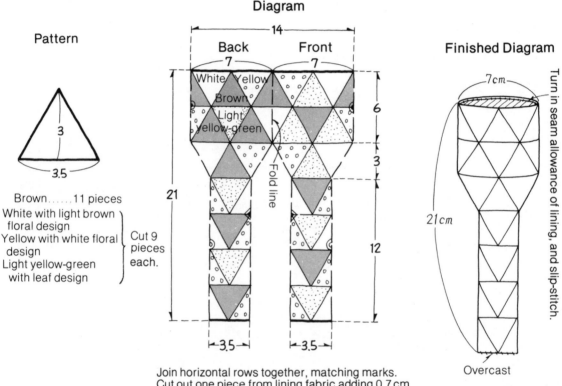

Pattern

Brown......11 pieces
White with light brown floral design
Yellow with white floral design
Light yellow-green with leaf design } Cut 9 pieces each.

Diagram

Back   Front

Finished Diagram

Join horizontal rows together, matching marks.
Cut out one piece from lining fabric adding 0.7 cm seam allowance same size as top piece.

35 Sewing Case shown on page 25

MATERIALS: Cotton fabrics: brown with white checks, 90 cm by 15 cm; red-brown, 15 cm by 10 cm; olive green, 12 cm by 6 cm; white with floral design, 9 cm by 10 cm; fabric for lining, 24 cm by 12 cm. #30 white cotton thread. Quilt batting, 24 cm by 12 cm. Adhesive interlining, 12 cm by 11 cm. Cardboard, 20 cm by 22 cm. Glue.
FINISHED SIZE: See diagram.
DIRECTIONS: 1. Cut out pieces adding seam allowance or margin as indicated. Join pieces for front as shown in the illustration. Appliqué pieced

flower to front in slip stitch. Sew strip in place. 2. Pin and baste front, batting and lining together. Quilt as indicated. Glue quilted front to cardborad. 3. Place adhesive interlining on wrong side of pocket and press. Fold pocket as shown. Sew pocket in place. Sew strip for holder in place. Glue inner piece to cardboard. 4. Sew another strip to outer piece. With wrong sides of inner and outer pieces together, slip-stitch folded edge to outer piece all around.

Diagram

Add 0.7 cm seam allowance unless otherwise indicated.

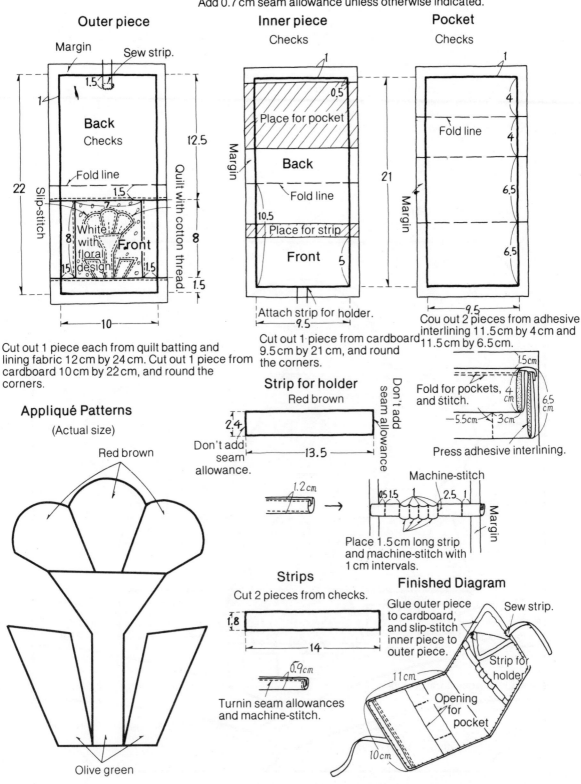

Outer piece

Margin

Sew strip.

1.5 1.4

Back

Checks

Fold line

1.5

White with floral design

Front

8

1.5

1.5

22

Slip-stitch

12.5

Quilt with cotton thread.

8

1.5

1

10

Cut out 1 piece each from quilt batting and lining fabric 12 cm by 24 cm. Cut out 1 piece from cardboard 10 cm by 22 cm, and round the corners.

Inner piece

Checks

0.5

Place for pocket

Back

Margin

Fold line

10.5

Place for strip

Front

5

21

Margin

Attach strip for holder.

9.5

Cut out 1 piece from cardboard 9.5 cm by 21 cm, and round the corners.

Pocket

Checks

4

Fold line

4

6.5

6.5

Margin

9.5

Cou out 2 pieces from adhesive interlining 11.5 cm by 4 cm and 11.5 cm by 6.5 cm.

1.5 cm

Fold for pockets, and stitch.

4 cm

6.5 cm

5.5 cm

3 cm

Press adhesive interlining.

Appliqué Patterns

(Actual size)

Red brown

Olive green

Strip for holder

Red brown

2.4

Don't add seam allowance.

13.5

Don't add seam allowance

1.2 cm

→

Machine-stitch

0.5 1.5 1   2.5 1

Margin

Place 1.5 cm long strip and machine-stitch with 1 cm intervals.

Strips

Cut 2 pieces from checks.

1.8

14

0.9 cm

Turnin seam allowances and machine-stitch.

Finished Diagram

Glue outer piece to cardboard, and slip-stitch inner piece to outer piece.

Sew strip.

Strip for holder

11 cm

Opening for pocket

10 cm

75

33 Sewing Box shown on page 25

MATERIALS: Cotton fabrics: brown with floral design, 84 cm by 40 cm; dark brown with floral design, 80 cm by 30 cm; mint ivory, 16 cm by 7 cm; white, 13 cm square; green with white floral design, 10 cm by 7 cm; small amount each of brick, brown, cream, beige, yellow-green, mustard, yellow with white floral design, white with green leaf design, beige with white floral design, white with red leaf design; fabric for lining, 26 cm square. #30 cotton thread: white; brown. #50 cotton thread in colors to match appliqués. Cardboard box (see diagram for size). Quilt batting, 80 cm by 35 cm. Cardboard, 60 cm by 32 cm. Glue.

FINISHED SIZE: Same size as box.
DIRECTIONS: 1. Cut out appliqué pieces adding 0.7 cm seam allowance. Sew pieces together using slip stitch in numerical order. 2. Cut out pieces for border adding seam allowance. Overcast pieces together by hand, placing cardboard shape on wrong side of each piece. 3. Make up for lid, following directions 1 through 3. 4. Cut out pieces from lining fabric, batting and cardboard. Make up for box, following directions for box.

Appliqué Patterns (Actual size)

1 strand in white
2 strands in brown } Quilt with cotton thread.

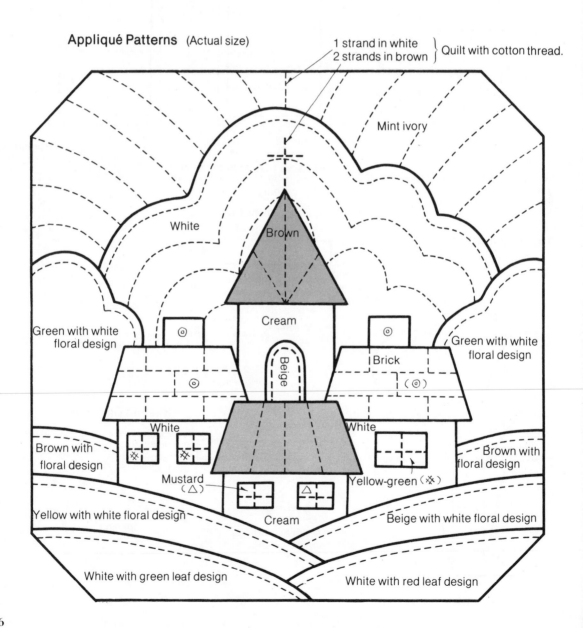

Mint ivory

White

Brown

Cream

Green with white floral design

Green with white floral design

Brick

Beige

White

White

Brown with floral design

Brown with floral design

Mustard (△)

Yellow-green (※)

Yellow with white floral design

Cream

Beige with white floral design

White with green leaf design

White with red leaf design

Patterns

3

3.5

Cut 12 pieces from brown with floral design fabric.

3.5

Cut 8 pieces from dark brown with floral design fabric.

Quilt with 1 strand of cotton thread in white.

(Actual size)

Cut 4 pieces from dark brown With floral design fabric.

Quilt with 1 strand of cotton thread in white.

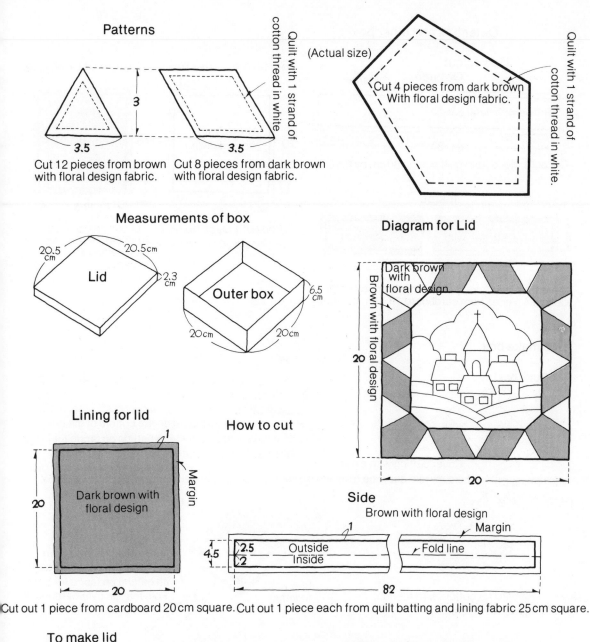

Measurements of box

20.5 cm   20.5 cm

Lid   2.3 cm

Outer box   6.5 cm

20 cm   20 cm

Diagram for Lid

Dark brown with floral design

Brown with floral design

20

20

Brown with floral design

Lining for lid

1

20   Margin

Dark brown with floral design

20

How to cut

Side

Brown with floral design

1   Margin

4.5   2.5 Outside
2 Inside   Fold line

82

Cut out 1 piece from cardboard 20 cm square. Cut out 1 piece each from quilt batting and lining fabric 25 cm square.

To make lid

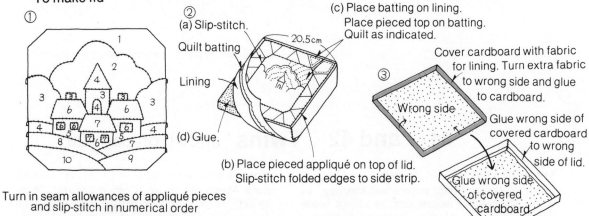

①

1
2
4
3   3   3   3
6   4   6
4   7   4
4   5   7 6 7   5   4
8   7
10   9

Turn in seam allowances of appliqué pieces and slip-stitch in numerical order with cotton thread in matching color.

② (a) Slip-stitch.

Quilt batting

Lining

(d) Glue.

20.5 cm

(b) Place pieced appliqué on top of lid. Slip-stitch folded edges to side strip.

(c) Place batting on lining. Place pieced top on batting. Quilt as indicated.

Cover cardboard with fabric for lining. Turn extra fabric to wrong side and glue to cardboard.

③

Wrong side

Glue wrong side of covered cardboard to wrong side of lid.

Glue wrong side of covered cardboard.

Outer box and inner box

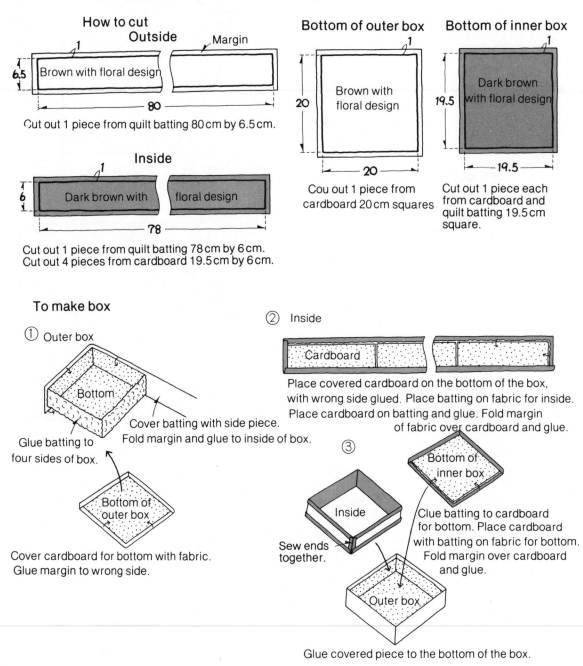

How to cut
Outside

6.5 — 1 — Brown with floral design — Margin

— 80 —

Cut out 1 piece from quilt batting 80 cm by 6.5 cm.

Inside

6 — 1 — Dark brown with floral design

— 78 —

Cut out 1 piece from quilt batting 78 cm by 6 cm.
Cut out 4 pieces from cardboard 19.5 cm by 6 cm.

Bottom of outer box

20 — 1 — Brown with floral design — 20

Cou out 1 piece from cardboard 20 cm squares

Bottom of inner box

19.5 — 1 — Dark brown with floral design — 19.5

Cut out 1 piece each from cardboard and quilt batting 19.5 cm square.

To make box

① Outer box

Bottom

Cover batting with side piece. Fold margin and glue to inside of box.

Glue batting to four sides of box.

Bottom of outer box

Cover cardboard for bottom with fabric. Glue margin to wrong side.

② Inside

Cardboard

Place covered cardboard on the bottom of the box, with wrong side glued. Place batting on fabric for inside. Place cardboard on batting and glue. Fold margin of fabric over cardboard and glue.

③

Bottom of inner box

Inside

Sew ends together.

Glue batting to cardboard for bottom. Place cardboard with batting on fabric for bottom. Fold margin over cardboard and glue.

Outer box

Glue covered piece to the bottom of the box.

41 and 42 Twins shown on page 29

MATERIALS: For each doll: apricot pink jersey, 82 cm by 14 cm; unbleached sheeting, 44 cm by 12 cm; white looped yarn; two black beads (large); two pairs of snap fasteners (medium); polyester fiberfill; orange felt-tipped pen. For 41:

Cotton fabrics: pink, 48 cm by 15 cm; old rose with floral design, 44 cm by 16 cm; red-brown, 38 cm by 8 cm; beige with floral design, ivory with floral design, white with pink stripes, 27 cm by 8 cm each; white, 18 cm by 9 cm; salmon pink, 18 cm by 8 cm.

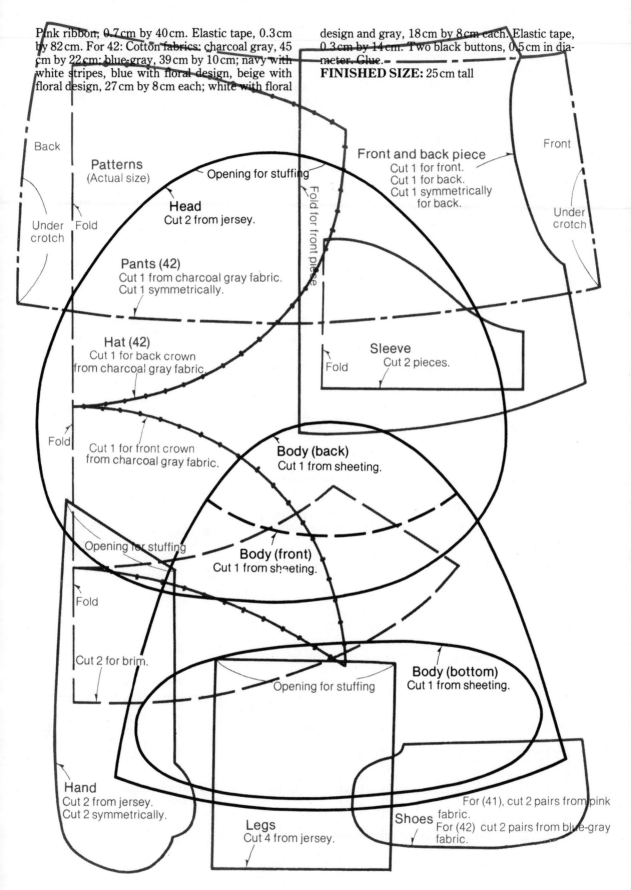

Pink ribbon, 0.7cm by 40cm. Elastic tape, 0.3cm by 82cm. For 42: Cotton fabrics: charcoal gray, 45 cm by 22cm; blue-gray, 39cm by 10cm; navy with white stripes, blue with floral design, beige with floral design, 27cm by 8cm each; white with floral design and gray, 18cm by 8cm each. Elastic tape, 0.3cm by 14cm. Two black buttons, 0.5cm in diameter. Glue.

FINISHED SIZE: 25cm tall

Back

Under crotch

Fold

Patterns
(Actual size)

Opening for stuffing

Fold for front piece

Head
Cut 2 from jersey.

Pants (42)
Cut 1 from charcoal gray fabric.
Cut 1 symmetrically.

Hat (42)
Cut 1 for back crown
from charcoal gray fabric.

Fold

Cut 1 for front crown
from charcoal gray fabric.

Front and back piece
Cut 1 for front.
Cut 1 for back.
Cut 1 symmetrically
for back.

Front

Under crotch

Fold

Sleeve
Cut 2 pieces.

Body (back)
Cut 1 from sheeting.

Opening for stuffing

Body (front)
Cut 1 from sheeting.

Fold

Cut 2 for brim.

Opening for stuffing

Body (bottom)
Cut 1 from sheeting.

Hand
Cut 2 from jersey.
Cut 2 symmetrically.

Legs
Cut 4 from jersey.

Shoes
For (41), cut 2 pairs from pink fabric.
For (42) cut 2 pairs from blue-gray fabric.

Directions: For 41:

① Cut out pieces adding 0.7 cm seam allowance. With right sides facing, stitch pieces together to make head, arms and legs.

Opening for stuffing
Head

Arms

② Turn to right side. Stuff with polyester fiberfill.

Sew opening closed.

Run a gathering stitch along top edges of arms and legs.

③ With right sides of front and back of the body together and arms in between, stitch each side. Sew bottom piece to body.

2.5 cm
4 cm
Bottom
Seam allowance

Leg
Shoe
Sew together.

⑤ Sew head to body.

⑥ Cut out two pieces for bloomers adding 0.7 cm seam allowance. With right sides together, stitch each side. Sew elastic tape to top and bottom.

Bloomers
Cut 2 from white fabric.
7
8   2
16

④ Stuff body with polyester fiberfill.

Pull thread of gathering stitch a little and turn in seam allowances of legs. Sew legs to body.

Turn in seam allowance of body

⑦ Make skirt in same manner as for bloomers.

Skirt
Cut 2 from red brown fabric.
6
17

Sew 18 cm long elastic tape in same manner as bloomers.

Turn in seam allowance, and machine-stitch.

16 cm long elastic tape

Turn in seam allowances, and machine-stitch.

Wrong side

Sew elastic tape by machine.

4.5 cm long elastic tape

⑧ Cut out pieces (a) through (f) adding seam allowance. Join pieces together by machine. Place patterns for dress on patched piece. Cut out one front, two back pieces, right and left sleeves adding 0.7 cm seam allowance.

Sleeves

Right	Left
b e f d	e f b d

5.5
3   12   12

Back piece

| a | b | c | | d | c | f |
| b | c | d | | e | f | a |

12.5
3   9   3   9

Front piece

| a | b | c | d | e | f |
| b | c | d | e | f | a |

3
18

a = Red brown
b = Beige with floral design
c = Salmon pink
d = Old-rose with floral design
e = Ivory with floral design
f = Pink with white stripes

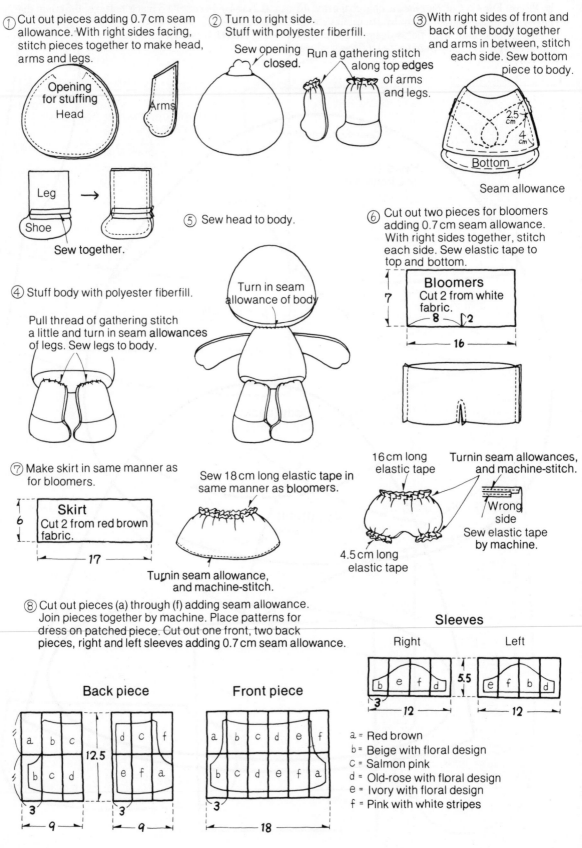

Sew sleeves to front and back.

Cut out pieces for hat adding 0.7 cm seam allowance. Join pieces together. Sew hat to head.

Turn in seam allowance, and machine-stitch.

Front

Sew 14 cm long elastic tape by machine.

Tie 16 cm ribbon to bow and sew in place.

Hat

13

Cut 2 from pink fabric.
Cut 2 from oldrose with floral design fabric.

13

Floral design | Pink
Sew 4 pieces together.
Pink | Floral design

4 cm

Back

1.5 cm

Attach snap fasteners

Turn in seam allowance, and machine-stitch.

Sew hat to head at position of elastic tape

Tack 25 cm long elastic tape to inside of hat, and machine-stitch.

Finished Diagram

⑪ Make curly hair with looped yarn. Sew hair to head.

Dowel

2 cm

Wind 6 times.

Fasten

Make 12 loops and sew them around forehead.

Tie 12 cm long ribbon to bow and glue to hair.

25 cm

Sew on beads.

Rouge

Nose

Polyester fiberfill

Gathering stitch

Jersey 3 cm in diameter

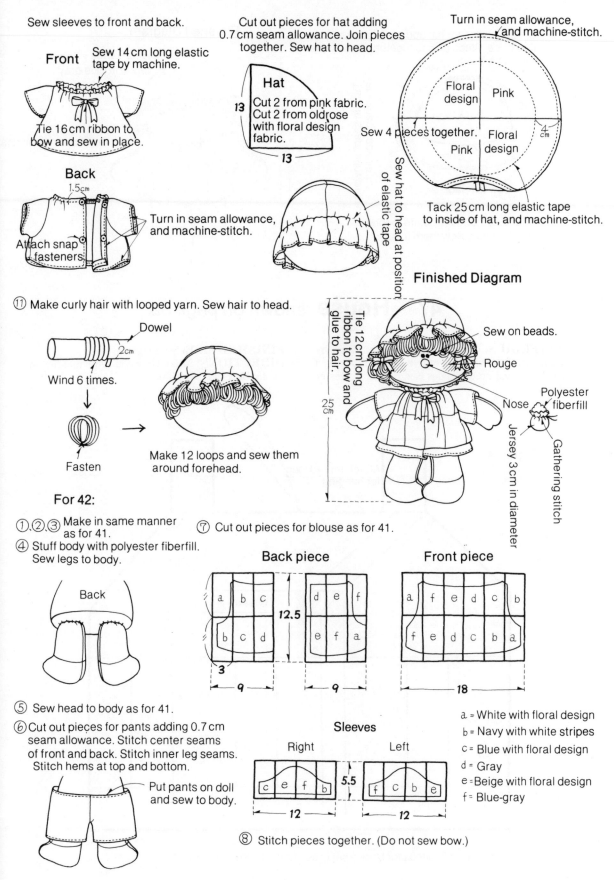

For 42:

①,②,③ Make in same manner as for 41.

④ Stuff body with polyester fiberfill. Sew legs to body.

⑦ Cut out pieces for blouse as for 41.

Back

Back piece

a	b	c		d	e	f
b	c	d		e	f	a

12.5

3

9 — 9

Front piece

a	f	e	d	c	b
f	e	d	c	b	a

18

⑤ Sew head to body as for 41.

⑥ Cut out pieces for pants adding 0.7 cm seam allowance. Stitch center seams of front and back. Stitch inner leg seams. Stitch hems at top and bottom.

Put pants on doll and sew to body.

Sleeves

Right

c	e	f	b

Left

f	c	b	e

5.5

12 12

a = White with floral design
b = Navy with white stripes
c = Blue with floral design
d = Gray
e = Beige with floral design
f = Blue-gray

⑧ Stitch pieces together. (Do not sew bow.)

⑨ Cut out pieces for hat adding 0.7 cm seam allowance. Stitch pieces together to make hat. Put hat on head.

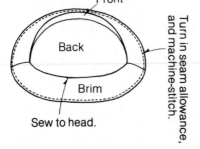

Front

Back

Brim

Sew to head.

Turn in seam allowance, and machine-stitch.

⑩ Make 19 loops with white looped yarn for hair. Sew them to head.

Finished Diagram

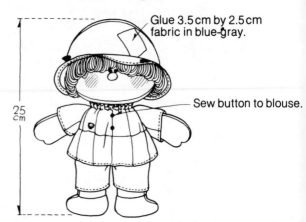

Glue 3.5 cm by 2.5 cm fabric in blue-gray.

25 cm

Sew button to blouse.

47 House shown on page 32

MATERIALS: Cotton fabrics: green, 27 cm by 13 cm; small amount each of five different prints in red shades and green shades (see photo). Polyester fiberfill.

FINISHED SIZE: See diagram.
DIRECTIONS: Make House in same manner as for 45: Star (see page 35).

Patterns
(Actual size)

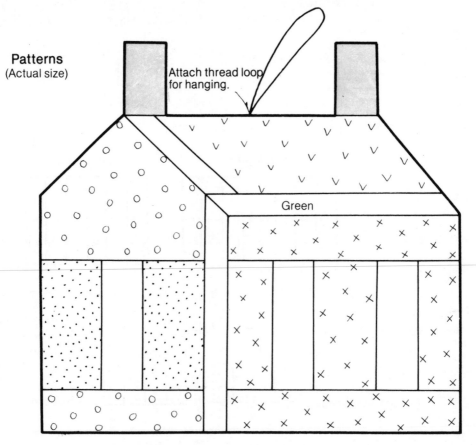

Attach thread loop for hanging.

Green

Cut out patch pieces for back from green fabric same size as front.

48 Christmas Wreath shown on page 33

MATERIALS: Cotton fabrics: red with white dots, 84 cm by 42 cm; ivory, 65 cm by 17 cm. Green bias binding tape, 4.5 cm by 150 cm. Red bias binding tape, 1.8 cm by 12 cm. Kapok.
FINISHED SIZE: 37 cm in diameter

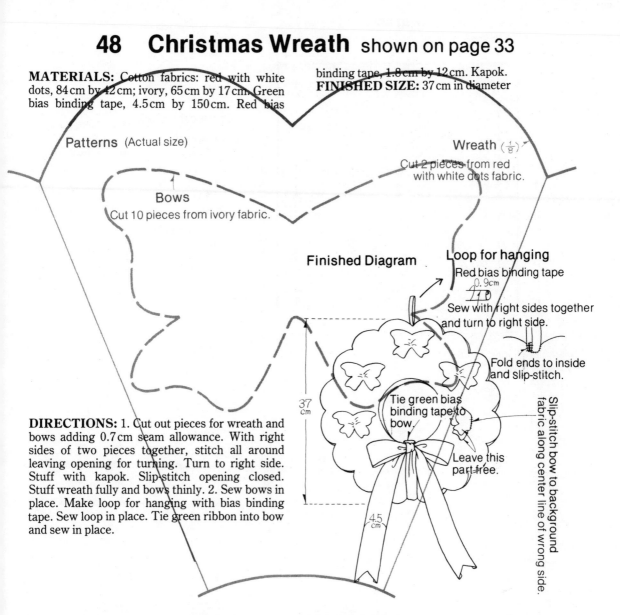

Patterns (Actual size)

Bows
Cut 10 pieces from ivory fabric.

Wreath ($\frac{1}{8}$)
Cut 2 pieces from red with white dots fabric.

Finished Diagram

Loop for hanging
Red bias binding tape
0.9 cm
Sew with right sides together and turn to right side.

Fold ends to inside and slip-stitch.

Tie green bias binding tape to bow.

37 cm

4.5 cm

Leave this part free.

Slip-stitch bow to background fabric along center line of wrong side.

DIRECTIONS: 1. Cut out pieces for wreath and bows adding 0.7 cm seam allowance. With right sides of two pieces together, stitch all around leaving opening for turning. Turn to right side. Stuff with kapok. Slip-stitch opening closed. Stuff wreath fully and bows thinly. 2. Sew bows in place. Make loop for hanging with bias binding tape. Sew loop in place. Tie green ribbon into bow and sew in place.

49 Cathedral Window Wall Hanging shown on page 36

MATERIALS: Cotton fabrics: navy, 46 cm by 92 cm; ivory with big purple floweres, 31 cm square; ivory with small purple flowers, 90 cm by 58 cm; unbleached sheeting, 90 cm by 18 cm; heavyweight cotton fabric in navy for background, 54 cm square. Polyester fiberfill. Wooden dowel, 1.2 cm in diameter and 55 cm long. Glue.
FINISHED SIZE: 52 cm square
DIRECTIONS: 1. Cut out pieces for Cathedral Window blocks and puffs. 2. Following directions for making Cathedral Window on page 39, make four blocks of 4 squares. Glue pieced blocks to navy cotton fabric. 3. With wrong sides of front and back pieces for puff together, stitch all around, making pleats on each side. Make a slash on back of each puff. Stuff with polyester fiberfill. Over-cast the slash closed. 4. Place Cathedral Window blocks on navy for background, matching centers. Slip-stitch in large stitches. Slip-stitch puffs around Cathedral Window blocks. Turn in seam allowance of background fabric. Slip-stitch pieced top to background. Attach wooden dowel.

Diagram

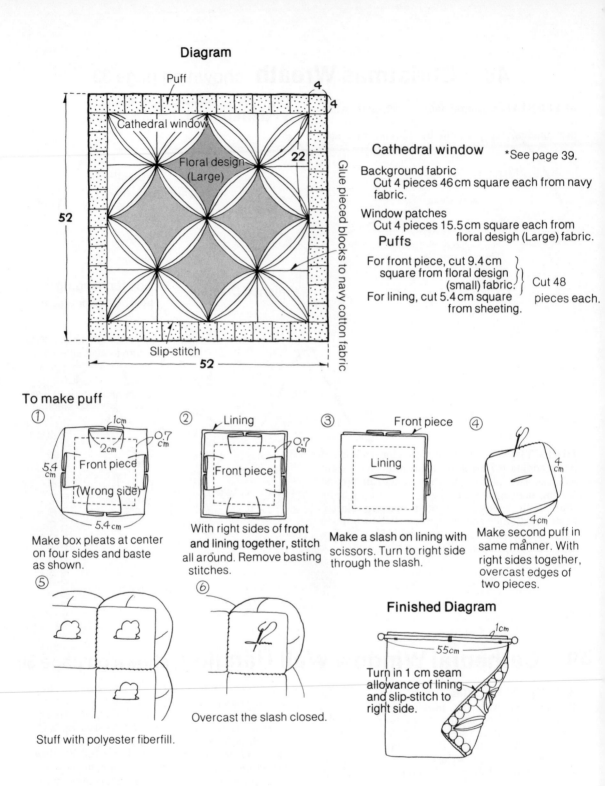

Puff

4
4

Cathedral window

Floral design
(Large)

22

52

52

Glue pieced blocks to navy cotton fabric

Slip-stitch

Cathedral window   *See page 39.

Background fabric
  Cut 4 pieces 46 cm square each from navy
  fabric.

Window patches
  Cut 4 pieces 15.5 cm square each from
  floral desigh (Large) fabric.
  Puffs

For front piece, cut 9.4 cm
  square from floral design
  (small) fabric.   } Cut 48
For lining, cut 5.4 cm square   pieces each.
  from sheeting.

To make puff

① 1cm 2cm 0.7cm
  5.4cm
  Front piece
  (Wrong side)
  5.4 cm

Make box pleats at center
on four sides and baste
as shown.

② Lining
  Front piece
  0.7cm

With right sides of front
and lining together, stitch
all around. Remove basting
stitches.

③ Front piece
  Lining

Make a slash on lining with
scissors. Turn to right side
through the slash.

④ 4cm
  4cm

Make second puff in
same manner. With
right sides together,
overcast edges of
two pieces.

⑤

⑥

Overcast the slash closed.

Stuff with polyester fiberfill.

Finished Diagram

1cm
55cm

Turn in 1 cm seam
allowance of lining
and slip-stitch to
right side.

51—52 **Pieced Star Pillows** shown on page 40

MATERIALS: For 51: Cotton fabrics: red, 46
cm by 42cm; red with dots and vermilion with
floral design, 52 cm by 26cm each. For 52: Cotton
fabrics: yellow-brown, 85 cm by 42cm; navy with

white floral design, 52 cm by 26cm. 34 cm long
zipper. Inner pillow stuffed with kapok, 43 cm
square.

FINISHED SIZE: 40 cm square.

DIRECTIONS: 1. Cut out 16 patch pieces each from dotted red and vermilion print adding seam allowance. Overcast patch pieces together by hand, placing cardboard shape on wrong side of each piece. 2. Cut out two pieces for back. Sew zipper to back. With right sides of front and back together, stitch all around. Turn to right side. Insert inner pillow.

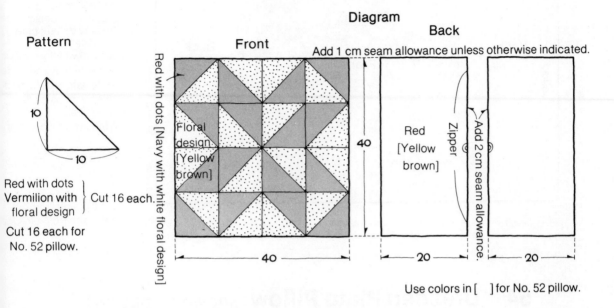

Pattern

10

10

Red with dots
Vermilion with floral design
} Cut 16 each.

Cut 16 each for
No. 52 pillow.

Red with dots [Navy with white floral design]

Diagram

Front

Back

Add 1 cm seam allowance unless otherwise indicated.

Floral design [Yellow brown]

40

40

Red [Yellow brown]

Zipper

Add 2 cm seam allowance.

20

20

Use colors in [ ] for No. 52 pillow.

53 Mosaic Pillow shown on page 40

MATERIALS: Cotton fabrics: pink, 87 cm by 26 cm; dark pink, 90 cm by 18 cm; white with red and green floral design, white with dark blue floral design, brown with floral design, white with red floral design, white with blue floral design, white with pale blue floral design, white with tulip design, 45 cm by 7 cm each; blue and yellow, 15 cm by 7 cm each. 36 cm long zipper. Cotton fabric for inner pillow, 90 cm by 46 cm. Kapok, 600 g.

FINISHED SIZE: 41.5 cm by 42 cm

DIRECTIONS: 1. Cut out hexagons and half-hexagons adding 0.7 cm seam allowance. Following Piecing Diagram, overcast patch pieces together by hand, placing cardboard shape on wrong side of each piece. 2. Cut out two pieces for front and back from pink fabric. Stitch pieces together. Place pieced hexagons on front and slip-stitch. Sew zipper to back. 3. With right sides of front and back together, stitch all around. Turn to right side. Insert inner pillow stuffed with kapok. (Piecing Diagram is shown on next page.)

Patterns (Actual size)

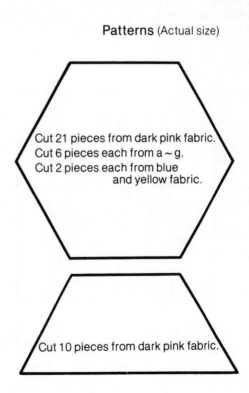

Cut 21 pieces from dark pink fabric.
Cut 6 pieces each from a ~ g.
Cut 2 pieces each from blue
and yellow fabric.

Cut 10 pieces from dark pink fabric.

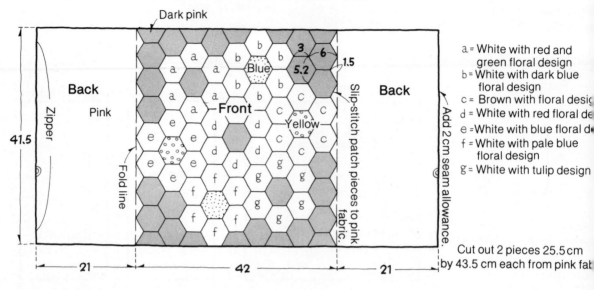

Dark pink

Back

Pink

Zipper

Fold line

Back

Slip-stitch patch pieces to pink fabric.

Add 2 cm seam allowance.

Front

Blue

Yellow

41.5

21 42 21

a = White with red and green floral design
b = White with dark blue floral design
c = Brown with floral design
d = White with red floral design
e = White with blue floral design
f = White with pale blue floral design
g = White with tulip design

Cut out 2 pieces 25.5 cm by 43.5 cm each from pink fabric

54 Dresden Plate Pillow shown on page 41

MATERIALS: Unbleached sheeting, 90 cm by 49 cm. Cotton prints (see photo for colors and designs), 20 pieces of 14 cm by 6.5 cm. #40 white cotton thread. 37 cm long zipper. Inner pillow stuffed with kapok, 45 cm square.
FINISHED SIZE: 43 cm square
DIRECTIONS: 1. Cut out patch pieces adding 0.7 cm seam allowance. Overcast patch pieces together by hand, placing cardboard shape on wrong side of each piece. 2. Cut out one piece for front from sheeting. Slip-stitch pieced patches to front. Hand-stitch on each patch piece with cotton thread. 3. Cut out two pieces for back. Sew zipper to back. With right sides of front and back together, stitch all around. Turn to right side. Insert inner pillow.

Front

Back

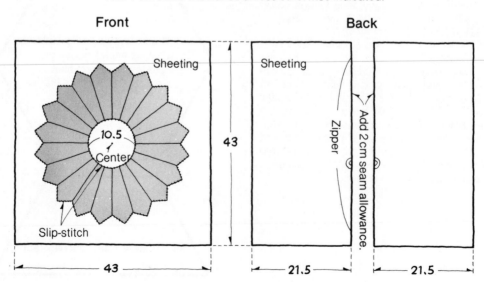

Sheeting

Sheeting

10.5

Center

Slip-stitch

Zipper

Add 2 cm seam allowance.

43

43 21.5 21.5

Pattern (Actual size)

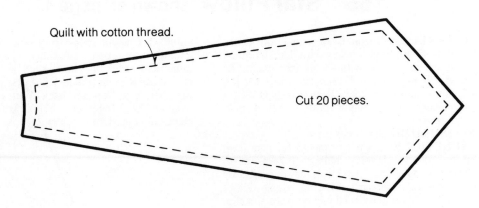

Quilt with cotton thread.

Cut 20 pieces.

56 Octagon and Square Pillow shown on page 41

MATERIALS: Cotton fabrics: blue, 76 cm by 48 cm; navy with white leaf design, 85 cm by 15 cm; navy with white floral design, 70 cm by 25 cm. 40 cm long zipper. Cotton fabric for inner pillow, 50 cm by 97 cm. Kapok, 600 g.
FINISHED SIZE: 45.5 cm square
DIRECTIONS: 1. Cut out patch pieces adding seam allowance. Overcast patch pieces together by hand, placing cardboard shape on wrong side of each piece. 2. Sew blue strips around pieced patches. Press seams to one side. 3. Sew back pieces together. Sew zipper to back. With right sides of front and back together, stitch all around. Turn to right side. Insert inner pillow stuffed with kapok.

Patterns

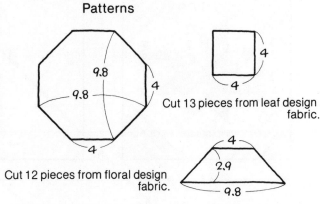

Cut 12 pieces from floral design fabric.

Cut 13 pieces from leaf design fabric.

Cut 12 pieces from leaf design fabric.

Diagram
Add 1 cm seam allowance unless otherwise indicated.

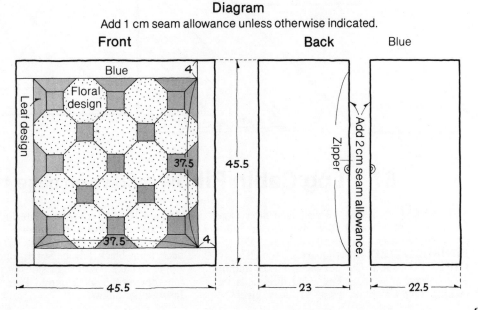

Front

Back

Blue

55 Star Pillow shown on page 41

MATERIALS: Cotton fabrics: emerald green, 90 cm by 49 cm; bright yellow with dots, 64 cm by 16 cm; emerald green with design (see photo), 38 cm by 19 cm for (a) and 32 cm by 16 cm for (b). #25 six-strand embroidery floss in yellow. 37 cm long zipper. Inner pillow stuffed with kapok, 45 cm square.

FINISHED SIZE: 43 cm square

DIRECTIONS: 1. Cut out pieces for star from bright yellow fabric, adding 0.7 cm seam allowance. Overcast patch pieces together by hand, placing cardboard shape on wrong side of each piece. 2. Center pieced star on front and slip-

stitch. 3. Cut out strips from fabrics (a) and (b), adding 1 cm seam allowance. Sew strips in numerical order. 4. Hand-stitch along seams of each piece with embroidery floss. Sew back pieces together. Sew zipper to back. With right sides of front and back together, stitch all around. Turn to right side. Insert inner pillow.

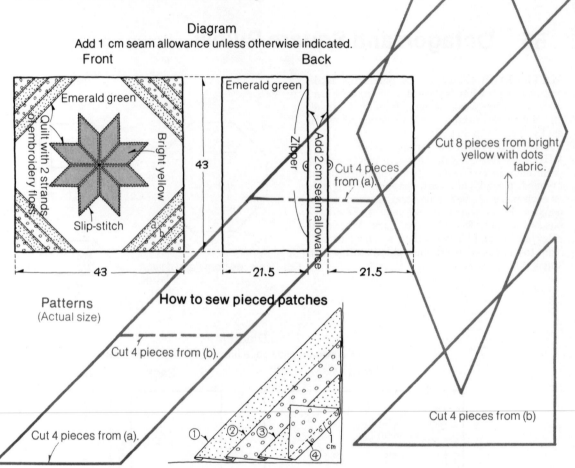

Diagram
Add 1 cm seam allowance unless otherwise indicated.

57 Log Cabin Pillow shown on page 41

MATERIALS: Cotton fabrics: (see next page for colors and amounts.) 36 cm long zipper. Inner pillow stuffed with kapok, 45 cm square.

FINISHED SIZE: 42 cm square

DIRECTIONS: 1. Cut out patch pieces adding 0.7 cm seam allowance. Following directions for making Log Cabin on page 11, sew pieces 1

through 16 to 23 cm square interlining. 2. Following Piecing Diagram for placement of colors, sew pieces together by hand. 3. Cut out two pieces for back from black fabric. Stitch together and sew zipper to back. With right sides of front and back together, stitch all around. Turn to right side. Insert inner pillow.

Patterns (Actual size)
Cut out 4 pieces **each**.

Diagram

Front

Back
Add 1 cm seam allowance unless otherwise indicated.

Black

Zipper

Add 2 cm seam allowance.

42

42

21

21

21

21

Block

Dark color

Light color

e d c b

a

f g h i

Cut out 4 pieces 23 cm spuare each from lining fabric.

e
d
c
b
f
g
h
i

21

21

Color key and required amounts of fabrics

		Color key	Required amounts
Prints in dark colors	a	Black with green and red flowers	24 cm × 6 cm
	b	Navy with white flowers	36 cm × 12 cm
	c	Black with red flowers	52 cm × 12 cm
	d	Olive green with white flowers	70 cm × 12 cm
	e	Black with white flowers	86 cm × 12 cm
Prints in light colors	f	Mustard with flowers	28 cm × 12 cm
	g	Gray with flowers	44 cm × 12 cm
	h	White with pink flowers	61 cm × 12 cm
	i	White with gray flowers	78 cm × 12 cm
		Black	48 cm × 44 cm
Lining		Unbleached sheeting	46 cm square

e

i . e

d . i

h 、d

c 、h

g 、c

b 、g

f 、b

f

a

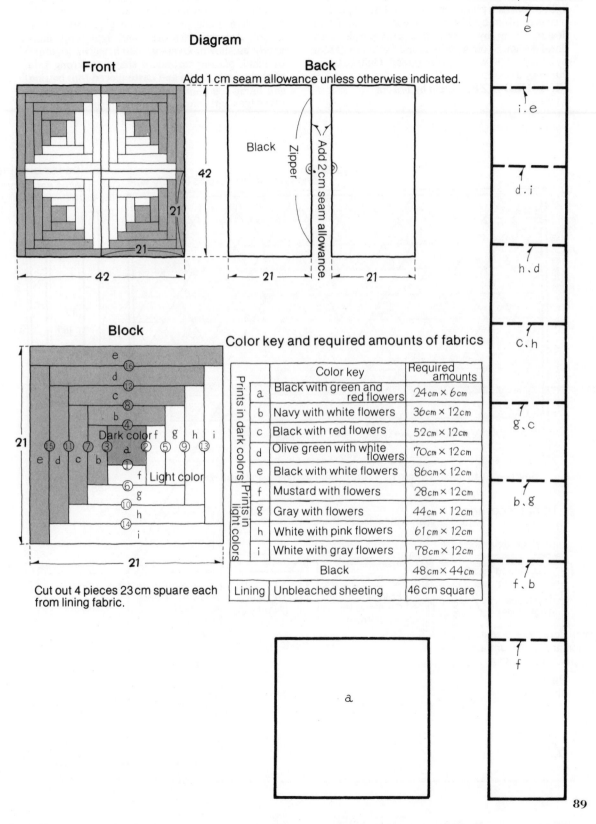

58 Thousand Pyramids Tablecloth shown on page 42

MATERIALS: Cotton fabrics: prints in dark and light colors (see photo for colors and designs), 243 pieces of 14 cm by 11.5 cm; olive green with floral design, 70 cm by 25 cm; dark gray-purple with floral design, 60 cm square; fabric for lining, 90 cm by 314 cm. #30 white cotton thread. Quilt batting, 90 cm by 314 cm.
FINISHED SIZE: 157 cm by 174 cm

DIRECTIONS: 1. Cut out patch pieces adding 0.7 cm seam allowance. Cut out 36 half-triangles from olive green print, reversing pattern for 18 pieces. Arrange dark print and light print alternately as shown. Overcast patch pieces together by hand, placing cardboard shape on wrong side of each piece. 2. Pin and baste pieced top, batting and lining together. Quilt on each triangle. Bind raw edges with bias-cut strips, mitering corners.

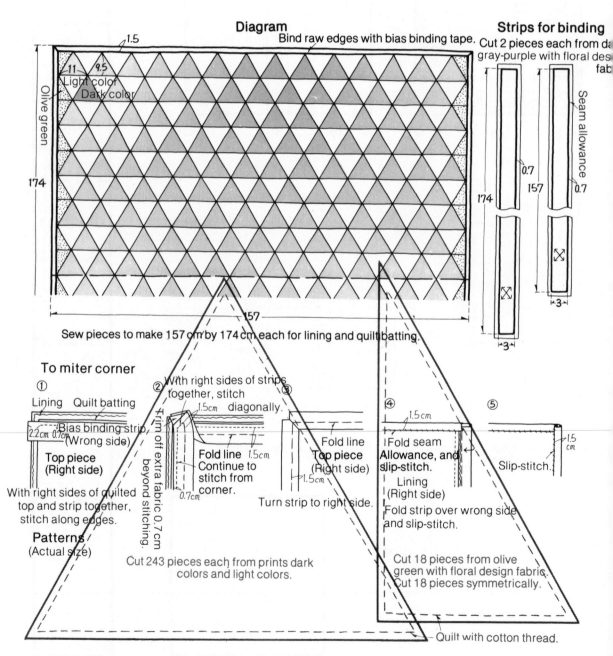

Diagram

Bind raw edges with bias binding tape.

1.5

11 9.5
Light color
Dark color

Olive green

174

157

Sew pieces to make 157 cm by 174 cm each for lining and quilt batting.

Strips for binding

Cut 2 pieces each from dark gray-purple with floral design fabric.

174   157

0.7   0.7

Seam allowance

3   3

3

To miter corner

① Lining   Quilt batting
Bias binding strip
(Wrong side)
2.2 cm 0.7 cm
Top piece
(Right side)
With right sides of quilted top and strip together, stitch along edges.

② With right sides of strips together, stitch diagonally.
Trim off extra fabric 0.7 cm beyond stitching.
1.5 cm
Fold line 1.5 cm
Continue to stitch from corner.
0.7 cm

③ Fold line
Top piece
(Right side)
1.5 cm
Turn strip to right side.

④ 1.5 cm
Fold seam Allowance, and slip-stitch.
Lining
(Right side)
Fold strip over wrong side and slip-stitch.

⑤ Slip-stitch.
1.5 cm

Patterns
(Actual size)

Cut 243 pieces each from prints dark colors and light colors.

Cut 18 pieces from olive green with floral design fabric. Cut 18 pieces symmetrically.

Quilt with cotton thread.

59 Mosaic Table Center shown on page 43

MATERIALS: Cotton fabrics and unbleached sheeting for top (see list below for colors and amounts); fabric for lining, 87 cm by 39 cm. #40 white cotton thread. Quilt batting, 87 cm by 39 cm.

FINISHED SIZE: 87 cm by 39 cm

DIRECTIONS: 1. Cut out patch pieces adding seam allowance. Overcast patch pieces together by hand, placing cardboard shape on wrong side of each piece. Trim off extra fabric of four sides leaving seam allowance. 2. Pin and baste pieced top, batting and lining together. Quilt on each piece. 3. Bind raw edges with bisa-cut strips. Sew long strips to top and bottom, then short ones to sides.

Patterns

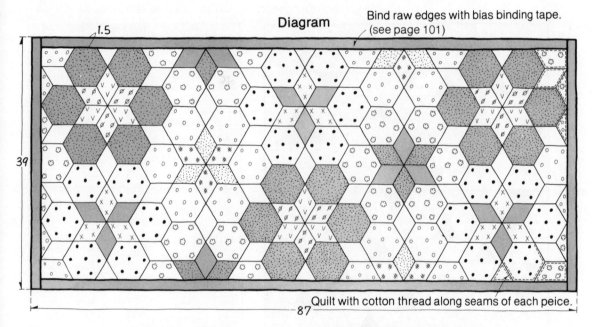

Diagram

Bind raw edges with bias binding tape. (see page 101)

Quilt with cotton thread along seams of each peice.

Cut out 1 piece each from lining fabric and quilt batting, 87 cm by 39 cm.

Color key and required amounts

Color key		Required pieces	Required amounts
	Navy with white flowers	◇ Cut 15 pieces	90 cm × 25 cm
		Cut 2 each for binding	
	Unbleached	◇ Cut 31 pieces	
		△ Cut 6 pieces	
	Red with white flowers	◯ Cut 18 pieces	81 cm × 25 cm
		◇ Cut 6 pieces	
	Yellow with white flowers	◯ Cut 17 pieces	
		◇ Cut 4 pieces	
	Gray with flowers	◯ Cut 17 pieces	
		◇ Cut 4 pieces	
	Blue with light blue flowers	◯ Cut 18 pieces	81 cm × 16 cm
	White with pink flowers		
	Ivory with red flowers	◇ Cut 9 pieces	50 cm × 9 cm
	White with blue flowers		
	Cream with leaves	◇ Cut 6 pieces	33 cm × 9 cm
	Olive green		

Strips for binding

Cut 2 pieces each.

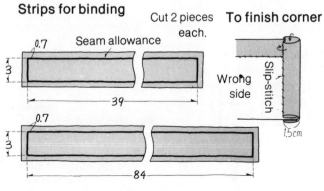

To finish corner

Wrong side

Slip-stitch

60
Thousand Pyramids Wall Hanging shown on page 44

MATERIALS: Cotton fabrics (see list for colors and amounts); fabric for lining, 81 cm by 95 cm.
FINISHED SIZE: 79 cm by 93 cm
DIRECTIONS: 1. Cut out patch pieces adding 0.7 cm seam allowance. Sew pieces together by hand, following Piecing Diagram. 2. Place pieced top on lining, turn in seam allowance and slip-stitch lining to hem 2-3 mm in from folded edge.

Pattern
(Actual size)

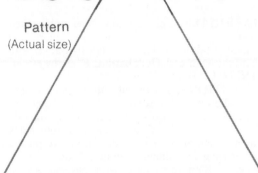

Diagram

Attach loop for hanging.

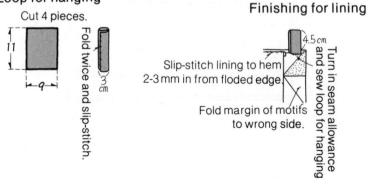

1

93

6.2

7.2

79.2

Color key and required amounts

Color key		Required pieces	Required amounts
	Navy	39	77 cm × 36 cm
		Loop 4	
	Black	36	72 cm × 27 cm
	Green	34	
	Yellow-green	33	66 cm × 27 cm
▲	Turquoise	29	88 cm × 18 cm
◎	Cobalt blue	24	72 cm × 18 cm
•	Mauve	22	66 cm × 18 cm
⊕	Pink with white dots		
※	Purple	21	
V	Pink		
○	Blue with white dots	18	55 cm × 18 cm
□	Cherry pink	9	55 cm × 9 cm
✿	Red with flowers	8	50 cm × 9 cm
	Red	7	44 cm × 9 cm
✦	Vermilion	6	39 cm × 9 cm
■	Orange	4	28 cm × 9 cm
◉	Orange with white dots		
△	Mandarin	3	22 cm × 9 cm
⋏	Bright yellow with white dots		
T	Yellow	2	17 cm × 9 cm

Loop for hanging

Cut 4 pieces.

11

9

3 cm

Fold twice and slip-stitch.

Finishing for lining

4.5 cm

Slip-stitch lining to hem 2-3 mm in from floded edge.

Fold margin of motifs to wrong side.

Turn in seam allowance and sew loop for hanging.

92

61 Ohio Star Quilt shown on page 45

MATERIALS: Cotton fabrics: olive green, 90 cm by 182 cm; brown with white flowers, 60 cm by 15 cm; fabrics for A (see samples below for placement of colors); fabric for lining, 92 cm by 252 cm. #40 white cotton thread. Two pieces of polyester batting.

FINISHED SIZE: 126 cm by 182 cm

DIRECTIONS: 1. Cut out patch pieces for A adding 0.7 cm seam allowance. Sew pieces together by hand, following photo and samples for placement of colors. Make 24 blocks. 2. Cut out pieces for B and C adding 0.7 cm seam allowance. Join A blocks together with B and C, following Piecing Diagram. 3. Sew strips for border around pieced top. Pin and baste pieced top, batting and lining together. Quilt on each patch piece of block A. 4. Bind raw edges with olive green strips.

Diagram

Sew pieces for lining 126 cm by 182 cm.

Strips for border

Cut 2 pieces each from olive green fabric.

0.7 Seam allowance

Strips for binding

Cut 2 pieces each from olive green fabric.

Bind raw edges with bias binding tape. (See page 101)

Following photo for placement of colors, arrange patches.

Patterns
(Actual size)

Blocks (Add 0.7 cm seam allowance)

A (Samples for placement of colors)

Quilt along seam lines.

▓ = 86 cm × 8 cm
☐ = 46 cm × 8 cm
⊠ = 14 cm × 7 cm

▓ = 42 cm × 7 cm
☐ = 46 cm × 8 cm
⊠ = 58 cm × 8 cm

▓ = 86 cm × 8 cm
☐ = 32 cm × 8 cm
⊠ ○ = 14 cm × 7 cm each

▓ = 44 cm × 8 cm
☐ = 48 cm × 8 cm
⊠ = 58 cm × 8 cm

▓ = 44 cm × 8 cm
☐ = 48 cm × 8 cm
⊠ = 58 cm × 8 cm

B
Cut 38 pieces from olive green fabric.

C
Cut 15 pieces from brown with white floral design fabric.

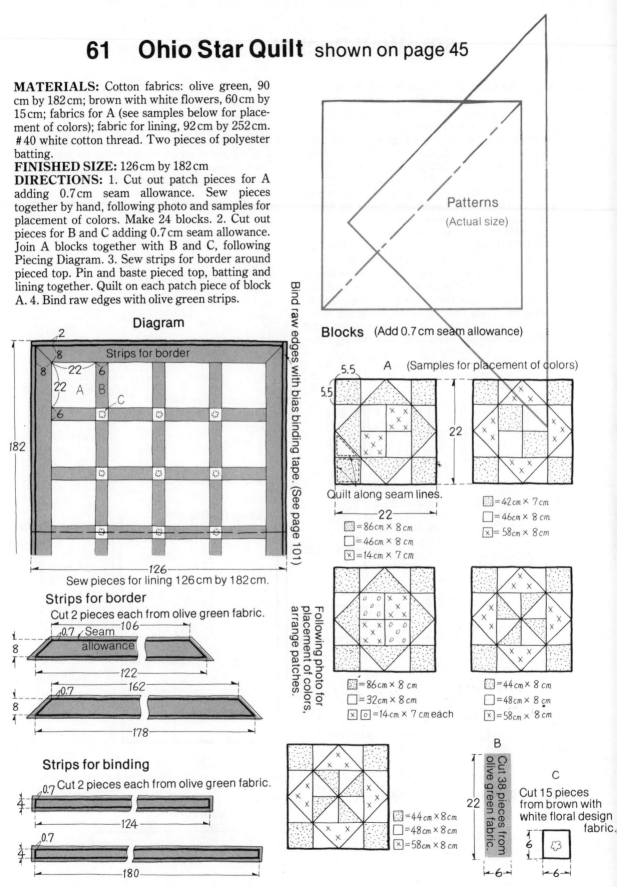

93

62 Wall Pockets shown on page 46

MATERIALS: Heavyweight cotton fabric in light brown, 40cm by 50cm. Cotton fabrics: purple and green, 70cm by 26cm each; yellow-green with floral design and gray-purple print, 29 cm by 10 cm each; orange, orange with white dots, white with design, red, pink with white dots, pink, wine red, red with floral design, 19cm by 10 cm each; fabric for lining, 80cm by 50cm. #25 six-strand embroidery floss in colors to match patches. Non-woven interlining, 63cm by 18cm. Adhesive interlining, 40cm by 49cm.

FINISHED SIZE: 40cm by 48.5cm

DIRECTIONS: 1. Cut out patch pieces for pockets A and B adding 0.7cm seam allowance. Sew pieces together by hand. 2. Place pockets A on non-woven interlining and quilt on each triangle. Quilt in same manner as for B. Place quilted pocket on lining and slip-stitch along top edge. Bind raw edges with strip. 3. Place background fabric on adhesive interlining and press. Place pocket B on background, turn over seam allowance of bottom to wrong side. Slip-stitch lining to seam allowance. 4. Turn over seam allowance of top to wrong side. Slip-stitch lining to seam allowance. Bind raw edges of each side with strip, extending end of strips to make loop for hanging. 5. Tack center of pocket B to background. Slip-stitch pockets A to background.

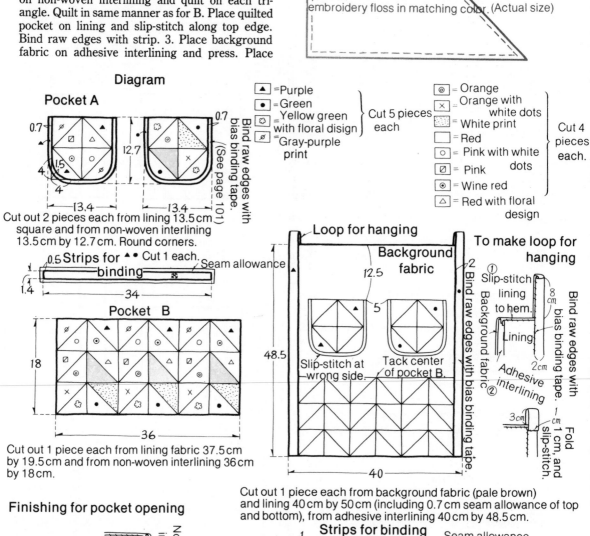

Pattern

Quilt with 2 strands of embroidery floss in matching color. (Actual size)

Diagram

Pocket A

0.7 0.7 12.7 (See page 101)

1.5 4 4

13.4 13.4

Bind raw edges with bias binding tape.

Cut out 2 pieces each from lining 13.5 cm square and from non-woven interlining 13.5cm by 12.7cm. Round corners.

▲ =Purple
● =Green
▣ =Yellow green with floral disign
∅ =Gray-purple print
} Cut 5 pieces each

◉ = Orange
× = Orange with white dots
░ = White print
□ = Red
○ = Pink with white dots
⊘ = Pink
◉ = Wine red
△ = Red with floral design
} Cut 4 pieces each.

Strips for ▲● Cut 1 each.
0.5 binding Seam allowance 25
1.4 34

Pocket B

18 36

Cut out 1 piece each from lining fabric 37.5cm by 19.5cm and from non-woven interlining 36cm by 18cm.

Loop for hanging

Background fabric 12.5 2 5 48.5

Slip-stitch at wrong side. Tack center of pocket B.

Bind raw edges with bias binding tape. Background fabric Adhesive interlining

40

Cut out 1 piece each from background fabric (pale brown) and lining 40cm by 50cm (including 0.7 cm seam allowance of top and bottom), from adhesive interlining 40cm by 48.5cm.

To make loop for hanging

① Slip-stitch lining to hem. 8 cm Lining 2cm

② Adhesive interlining 3cm 1cm 1cm

Bind raw edges with bias binding tape. Fold 1cm and slip-stitch.

Finishing for pocket opening

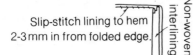

Slip-stitch lining to hem 2-3mm in from folded edge.

Non-woven interlining

Strips for binding

1 Seam allowance
4 ▲●Cut 1 each
55.5

63 Pillow Case and 64 Matching Border for Top Sheet shown on page 47

MATERIALS: For 63: Cotton fabrics: white, 72 cm by 112 cm; light blue, 90 cm by 49 cm. For 64: Cotton fabrics: light blue, 90 cm by 166 cm; white, 90 cm by 27 cm. #25 six-strand embroidery floss in pale blue and blue.

FINISHED SIZE: 63: 57 cm by 42 cm 64: 150 cm by 88 cm

DIRECTIONS: For 63: 1. Cut out appliqué and patch pieces adding 0.7 cm seam allowance. Sew patch pieces together, placing white piece on light blue. Appliqué and embroider as indicated. 2. Make double hem for opening of back pieces. Overlap back pieces and place on front, with right sides together. Stitch all around. Turn to right side. Stitch in the ditch along pieced border.

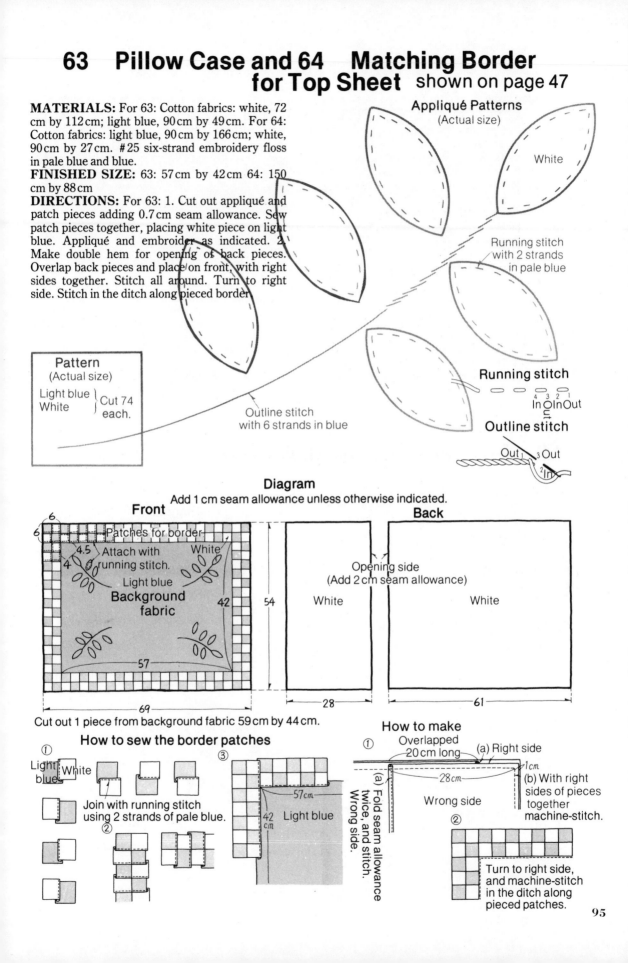

Appliqué Patterns
(Actual size)

White

Running stitch with 2 strands in pale blue

Running stitch

In O In Out
4 3 2 1

Outline stitch

Out 3 Out
In 2

Outline stitch with 6 strands in blue

Pattern
(Actual size)
Light blue }
White } Cut 74 each.

Diagram
Add 1 cm seam allowance unless otherwise indicated.

Front

Patches for border
4.5 Attach with running stitch.
White
Light blue
4
Background fabric
57
42
69

54

Back

Opening side
(Add 2 cm seam allowance)
White
White
28
61

Cut out 1 piece from background fabric 59 cm by 44 cm.

How to sew the border patches

① Light blue White

Join with running stitch using 2 strands of pale blue.

②

③ 57 cm
42 cm Light blue

How to make

① Overlapped 20 cm long
(a) Right side
28 cm
1 cm
(b) With right sides of pieces together machine-stitch

(a) Fold seam allowance twice, and stitch. Wrong side.

Wrong side

②
Turn to right side, and machine-stitch in the ditch along pieced patches.

95

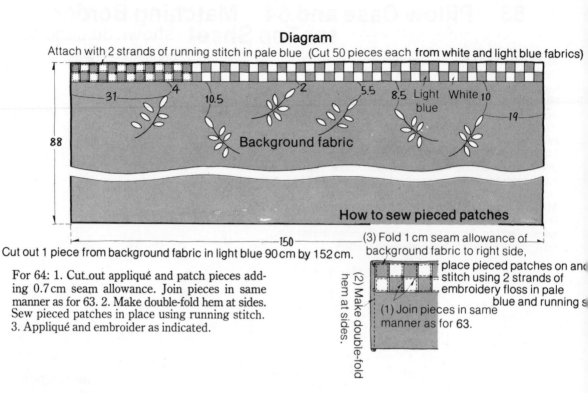

Diagram

Attach with 2 strands of running stitch in pale blue (Cut 50 pieces each from white and light blue fabrics)

31   4   10.5   2   5.5   8.5   Light blue   White 10   19

88   Background fabric

150

Cut out 1 piece from background fabric in light blue 90 cm by 152 cm.

For 64: 1. Cut_out appliqué and patch pieces adding 0.7 cm seam allowance. Join pieces in same manner as for 63. 2. Make double-fold hem at sides. Sew pieced patches in place using running stitch. 3. Appliqué and embroider as indicated.

How to sew pieced patches

(3) Fold 1 cm seam allowance of background fabric to right side, place pieced patches on and stitch using 2 strands of embroidery floss in pale blue and running s

(2) Make double-fold hem at sides.

(1) Join pieces in same manner as for 63.

68   Framed Patchwork Picture shown on page 48

MATEIRALS: Cotton fabrics: ivory print, 47 cm by 11 cm; green print, 20 cm by 12 cm; brown with floral design, 14 cm by 7 cm; fabric for lining, 16 cm in diameter. #50 white cotton thread. Quilt batting, 16 cm in diameter. Frame, 14 cm in inner diameter.
FINISHED SIZE: Same size as frame.
DIRECTIONS: 1. Cut out patch pieces adding 0.7 cm seam allowance. Sew pieces together by hand. 2. Pin and baste pieced top, batting and lining together. Quilt on each wedge piece along seam lines.
①
②

Diagram

Quilt on each wedge piece along seam lines with cotton thread.

14

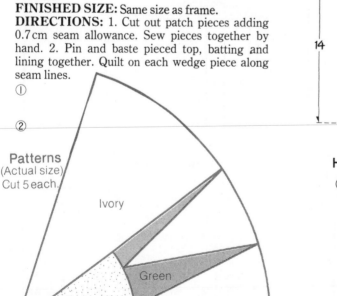

Patterns
(Actual size)
Cut 5 each.

Ivory

Green

Brown

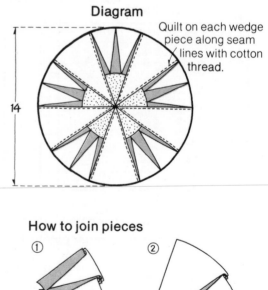

How to join pieces
①   ②

Join 5 pieces of (2)

65—67 Slippers shown on page 47

MATERIALS: (for one pair): Cotton fabrics: plain, 46 cm by 34 cm; print, 35 cm by 32 cm. Quilt batting, 53 cm by 21 cm.
FINISHED SIZE: Foot size, 26 cm.

DIRECTIONS: 1. Cut out pieces from plain and print fabrics adding 0.7 cm seam allowance. Sew each piece to quilt batting one after another, turning seams to one side. Make another upper piece, reversing placement of patches. 2. Cut out two soles from plain fabric. You may need a professional help for a finished slippers.

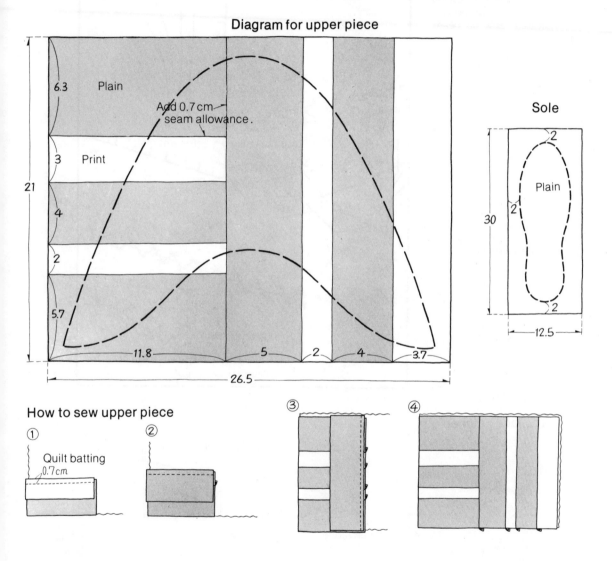

Diagram for upper piece

Plain

Add 0.7 cm seam allowance.

6.3
3 Print
4
2
5.7
21
11.8   5   2   4   3.7
26.5

Sole

Plain

2
2
2
2
30
12.5

How to sew upper piece

① Quilt batting 0.7 cm

②

③

④

69 Framed Crazy Quilt shown on page 48

MATERIALS: Cotton fabrics: apricot pink, 12 cm by 6 cm; lavender, 10 cm by 6 cm; ivory print, 9 cm by 7 cm; olive green, 8 cm by 5 cm; beige print, 5 cm square; fabric for lining, 16 cm by 11 cm.

Purple crepe, 12 cm by 5 cm. #25 six-strand embroidery floss in golden brown, wine red, navy, brown, drak brown, powder green, pink and olive green. Ivory cotton lace trim, 4 cm by 8 cm. 16

small beads in white. Quilt batting, 16cm by 11cm. Frame, 14cm by 9cm (inside measurement).

FINISHED SIZE: Same size as frame.

DIRECTIONS: 1. Cut out pieces adding 0.7cm seam allowance. Place batting on lining. Sew each piece to batting, stitching through all thicknesses. Place lace trim as indicated. 2. Embroider as indicated. Sew on beads in place.

Patterns (Actual size)

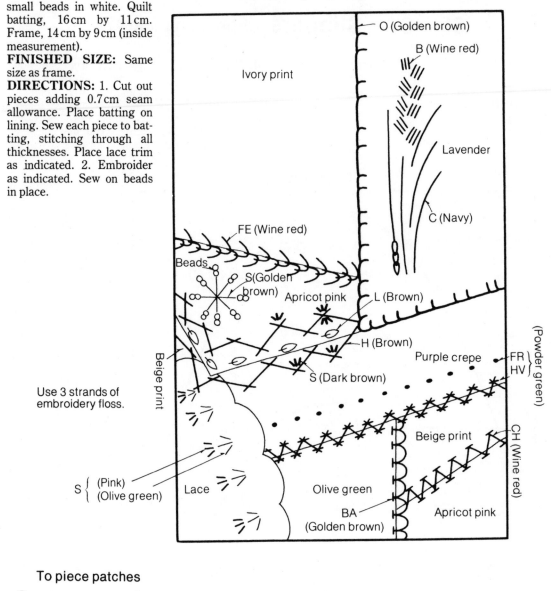

Use 3 strands of embroidery floss.

O (Golden brown)
B (Wine red)
Ivory print
Lavender
C (Navy)
FE (Wine red)
Beads
S (Golden brown)
Apricot pink
L (Brown)
H (Brown)
(Powder green)
Beige print
Purple crepe
FR
HV
S (Dark brown)
Beige print
CH (Wine red)
S { (Pink) (Olive green)
Lace
Olive green
Apricot pink
BA (Golden brown)

To piece patches

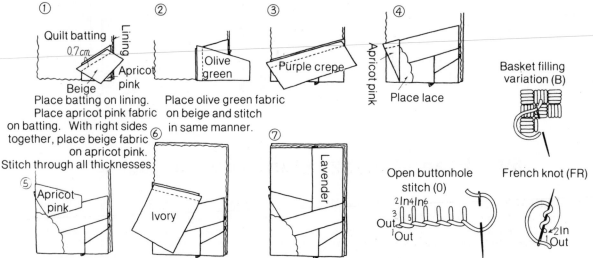

① Quilt batting 0.7cm Lining Apricot pink Beige pink
Place batting on lining. Place apricot pink fabric on batting. With right sides together, place beige fabric on apricot pink. Stitch through all thicknesses.

② Olive green
Place olive green fabric on beige and stitch in same manner.

③ Purple crepe

④ Apricot pink
Place lace

⑤ Apricot pink

⑥ Ivory

⑦ Lavender

Basket filling variation (B)

Open buttonhole stitch (0)
2 In 4 In 6
3 5
Out
1 Out

French knot (FR)
In
2 In
1 Out

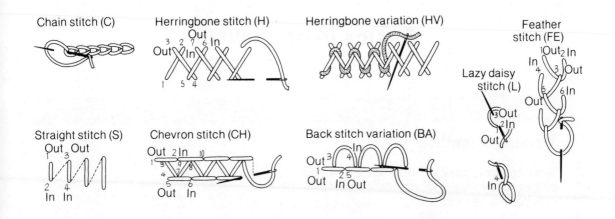

Chain stitch (C)

Herringbone stitch (H)

Herringbone variation (HV)

Feather stitch (FE)

Lazy daisy stitch (L)

Straight stitch (S)

Chevron stitch (CH)

Back stitch variation (BA)

70 Framed Patchwork Picture shown on page 48

MATERIALS: Cotton fabrics: light yellow-brown, 16 cm square; green, 7 cm square; prints (see photo), 8 pieces of 7 cm by 5 cm; golden brown, 4 cm in diameter; fabric for lining, 16 cm square. #50 white cotton thread. Quilt batting, 16 cm square. Frame, 14 cm square (inside measurement).
FINISHED SIZE: Same size as frame.

DIRECTIONS: 1. Cut out pieces adding 0.7 cm seam allowance. Appliqué stem, petals and stamen to light yellow-brown background. Arrange prints for petals, considering color harmony of the whole. 2. Pin and baste appliquéd top, batting and lining together. Quilt along quilting lines.

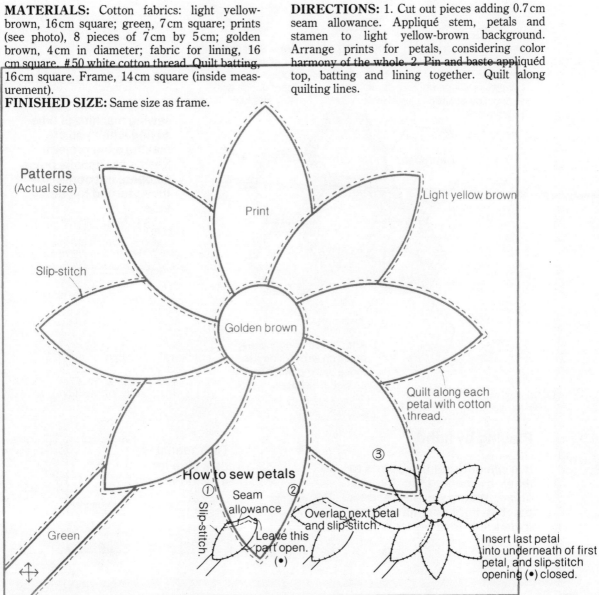

Patterns
(Actual size)

Light yellow brown

Print

Slip-stitch

Golden brown

Quilt along each petal with cotton thread.

③

How to sew petals

① Seam allowance

Slip-stitch.

②

Overlap next petal and slip-stitch.

Leave this part open. (•)

Green

Insert last petal into underneath of first petal, and slip-stitch opening (•) closed.

Basics in patchwork

Traditional method

Time and care may be required when you piece patches using this method, but you may have a neater finish.

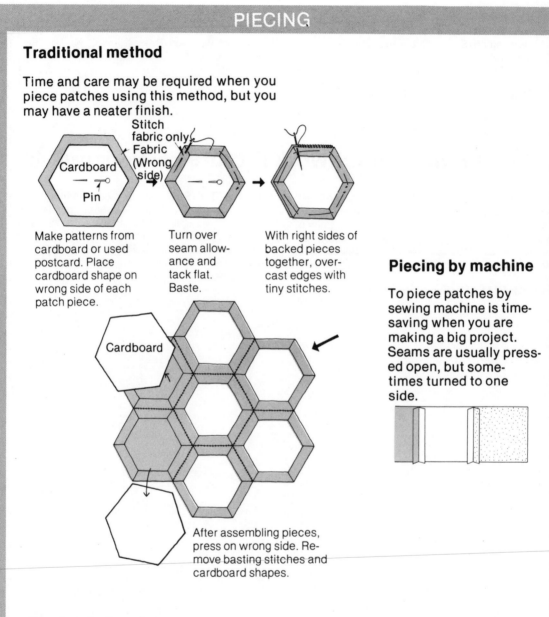

Make patterns from cardboard or used postcard. Place cardboard shape on wrong side of each patch piece.

Turn over seam allowance and tack flat. Baste.

With right sides of backed pieces together, overcast edges with tiny stitches.

After assembling pieces, press on wrong side. Remove basting stitches and cardboard shapes.

Piecing by machine

To piece patches by sewing machine is time-saving when you are making a big project. Seams are usually pressed open, but sometimes turned to one side.

Piecing by hand

It is easier to get tiny points to meet by hand than by machine. When you piece dark patch to light one, turn seams to dark side for a neater finish.

Turn seams to dark side for a neater finish.

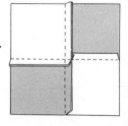

QUILTING

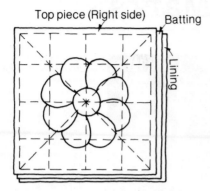

Pin and baste pieced top, batting and lining together. Quilt along quilting lines.

SLIP-STITCH (SIDE STITCH)

Seam allowance

Work vertically using matching thread with fabrics, showing very little stitches. (Work at curves, turning in seam allowance with needle.)

BINDING

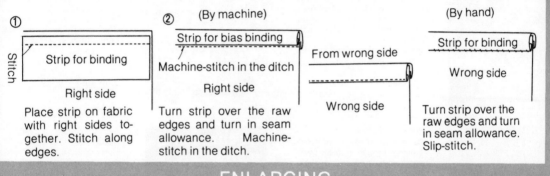

① Stitch / Strip for binding / Right side

Place strip on fabric with right sides together. Stitch along edges.

② (By machine) Strip for bias binding / Machine-stitch in the ditch / Right side

Turn strip over the raw edges and turn in seam allowance. Machine-stitch in the ditch.

From wrong side / Wrong side

(By hand) Strip for binding / Wrong side

Turn strip over the raw edges and turn in seam allowance. Slip-stitch.

ENLARGING

Make a tracing of original design. Then draw straight lines, horizontally and vertically, so that lines are equally patched in both ways. Use second paper with larger sections and number sections in same manner. Copy design from smaller squares.

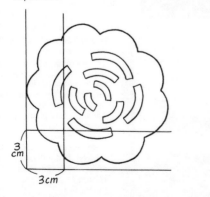

3 cm

3 cm

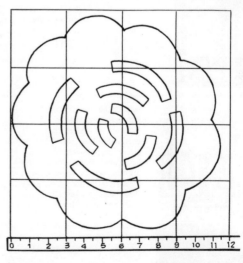

0 1 2 3 4 5 6 7 8 9 10 11 12

New Handicraft Books
with ONDORI Marks

GORGEOUS CROCHET LACES FOR INTERIOR DECORATION
Following the detailled illustrations and instructions, even the beginner can successfully create lace doilies, cushions, and tablecloths.
Among the wide range of patterns given are those for Italian and medieval European-style lace.
132 pp; $7\frac{1}{4} \times 10\frac{1}{4}$ in.
ISBN 487-3

CROCHET FOR THE HOME WITH COMPLETE DIAGRAMS
Crocheting lases to enhance your home is a popular hobby. Here are more than 30 elegant projects shown in color pictures. Tablecloths, doilies, piano throws, chair backs, bedspreads, etc., all worked in crochet cotton, are included with complete diagrams.
84 pp; $7\frac{1}{4} \times 10\frac{1}{4}$ in.
LC 80-84415
ISBN 495-4

THE EMBROIDERY OF ROSES
Here are patterns for roses from porcelain and clothes from the seventeenth to the nineteenth century, a ceremonial gown in Prague, a German baptismal shawl, a carpet woven in Milan, on Islamic glazed tiles from Turkey, and cut-paper works from traditional Chinese handicrafts.
Monograms incorporating the rose motif area also indicated.
144 pp; $7\frac{1}{4} \times 10\frac{1}{4}$ in.
ISBN 488-1

THE COLLECTION OF DESIGNS FOR CROSS-STITCH
Small and large flowers, scenes from fairy tales, geometric patterns and dolls are just a few of the designs that can be applied to tablecloths, cushions and other home items.
Many of the designs are given in their actual sizes, making it extremely easy. All designs are accompanied by illustrations to make this popular craft a cinch.
96 pp; $7\frac{1}{4} \times 10\frac{1}{4}$ in.
ISBN 486-5

HUCK EMBROIDERY
A modern version of huck embroidery. Includes cosmetic cases, pencil cases, book covers, bookmarks, purses, various kinds of bags, pillows and table linen. In addition, over 80 patterns for huck embroidery are shown in full color with charts.
This book will please any embroiderer who is curious about something different.
118 pp; $7\frac{1}{4} \times 10\frac{1}{4}$ in.
ISBN 519-5

THE COLLECTION OF STUFFED DOLLS FROM A FANCY WORLD
Here are step-by-step instructions for fifty marvelous dolls from the land of fantasy..... perfect gifts for a child, but a perfect inspiration, too, for groups working on bazaar or craft-fair projects. This book offers full-scale patterns and fully illustrated instructions for assembling all the cloth dolls, as well as knowing tips for the novice about handling this fabric or that.
156 pp; $7\frac{1}{4} \times 10\frac{1}{4}$ in.
ISBN 556-X

EMBROIDERY AND CROSS-STITCH FOR FRAMING
Here are 50 designs that make personalized art, for home or gift-giving, possible. There are landscapes, floral subjects, and nursery scenes to delight a child—everything from the three bears to a scené of windmills and duck pond. Meticulously detailed pattern pages make this beautiful needle art simple to create!
100 pp; $8\frac{1}{2} \times 10\frac{1}{4}$ in.
ISBN 537-3

ELEGANT CROSS-STITCH AND EMBROIDERY
This stunning collection of patterns to make in cross-stitch and traditional embroidery will beautify and home and provide never-to-be-forgotten gifts. There are bedsprads, runners, handbags, and tablecloths worked in patterns that range from handsome florals to a spritely Pennsylvania Dutch motif—60 designs in all.
112 pp; $8\frac{1}{2} \times 10\frac{1}{4}$ in.
ISBN 538-1